The Chicago Literary Experience

I0532147

The Chicago Literary Experience

Writing the City, 1893-1953

Frederik Byrn Køhlert

Museum Tusculanum Press
University of Copenhagen 2011

The Chicago Literary Experience: Writing the City, 1893–1953

© Museum Tusculanum Press and Frederik Byrn Køhlert, 2011
Copy editor: Jordy Findanis
Layout, composition and cover design: Pernille Sys Hansen, Damp Design
ISBN 978 87 635 3672 1

This book is published with financial support from
The Danish Research Council for the Humanities

Museum Tusculanum Press
126 Njalsgade
DK–2300 Copenhagen S
Denmark
www.mtp.dk

Contents

Acknowledgements

This book began its life as my MA thesis at Aarhus University, where it was composed under the enthusiastic and able guidance of Inger Hunnerup Dalsgaard. Since then, the manuscript has undergone several revisions, and I owe thanks to Russell Duncan at the University of Copenhagen and Sven H. Rossel at the University of Vienna for their insightful suggestions, as well as to Henry B. Wonham at the University of Oregon for his support and help with the comprehensive rewrite I worked on while I was a student of his. Mary Esteve at Concordia University provided the inspiration to seek out the material that serves as the subject for this book, and I am grateful to Signe Nielsen for her untiring help with procuring books and articles during the initial research stage. For their help with guiding the various drafts, thanks are due to Jordy Findanis and Johanna Skibsrud. I would like to express my gratitude to The Danish Research Council for the Humanities, whose financial support has made this publication possible. Finally, I would like to thank my family, Dorde, Kurt, Henrik, Lasse, Nanna and Valdemar for their continued support.

If you knew Chicago you'd talk about it too. If you haven't been in Chicago, you haven't been in the United States.

—Willard Motley

Find a writer who is indubitably an American in every pulse-beat, snort and adenoid, an American who has something new and peculiarly American to say and who says it in an unmistakable American way and nine times out of ten you will find that he has some sort of connection with the gargantuan and inordinate abattoir by Lake Michigan—that he was bred there, or got his start there or passed through there in days when he was young and tender.

—H. L. Mencken

This town of ours labors under one peculiar disadvantage: it is the only great city in the world to which all its citizens have come for the one common, avowed object of making money. There you have its genesis, its growth, its end and object.

—Henry B. Fuller

In Chicago, business comes first.
Coming in second, well,
that would be business.

—Billboard in O'Hare Airport, Chicago, 2004

_1_
Introduction
Looking for a Chicago Tradition

Almost all American cities have produced notable writers, and yet, as contemporary author Stuart Dybek writes, "one doesn't think about a Pittsburgh Tradition, or a St. Louis Tradition, an L.A. Tradition, or even a New York Tradition" (1993, xii). While his point is made with just a few examples, Dybek's list could go on while the implication slowly sinks in. If any American city is associated with a literary tradition, that city is Chicago. And yet this tradition is seldom carefully defined beyond the mention of a few names, such as Theodore Dreiser and James T. Farrell. But two writers do not make a literary tradition, and while Dreiser and Farrell share many characteristics, they are also widely different in terms of style and sentiment. What they do share, with each other and with many others, is a preoccupation with seeing the world from the point of view of characters who struggle through life and attempt to make sense of their peculiarly Chicagoan environment. And that, perhaps, is where any discussion of a Chicago Tradition should begin: With an attempt to understand the city itself—a city that, according to Dybek, "more than any other American city [...] draws its identity from its writers, and, in the process, imposes its identity upon them as well" (xi).

In *Lucy Gayheart*, the haunting 1935 novel about a young Nebraska girl's pursuit of art and love in Chicago, Willa Cather mentions how her tragic heroine, after some time in the city, "carried in her mind a very individual map of Chicago: a blur of smoke and wind and noise, with flashes of blue water, and certain clear outlines rising from the confusion […] This city of feeling rose out of the city of fact like a definite composition,—beautiful because the rest was blotted out" (20). When describing anything as complex as a city—even to one's self—the mind chooses certain features that come to represent the whole, constructing for each person a unique mental image that yields to interpretation and, in the case of Cather's Lucy, invests the essential abstractness of a sprawling metropolis like Chicago with definite meaning. Viewed this way, there are as many Chicagos as there are people, with each observer sorting the sensory impulses of the "city of fact" in a different way, as well as bringing an intensely personal perspective to the creation of yet another "city of feeling" from these raw materials. French philosopher Jean-Paul Sartre's Chicago, therefore, a "noble, lurid city, red as the blood that trickles through its abbatoirs, with its canals, the grey water of Lake Michigan and its streets crushed between clumsy and powerful buildings" (204), is very different from pioneering Chicago novelist Henry B. Fuller's city, which reminded him of "a pumpkin: it was big and sudden and coarse-textured" (1918, 63).

And yet there remains the Chicago of fact, out of which all representations must be shaped. Incorporated as a town in 1833, Chicago quickly grew to be a city of millions and was the birthplace of the skyscraper and the elevated railroad, as well as the large-scale corporations that came to dominate American business in the closing years of the nineteenth century. Reaching maturity with the 1893 World's Columbian Exposition, the city heralded the coming of the twentieth century and was emblematic of the new age of industrial capitalism that was replacing the traditional view of America as a garden to be cultivated by a nation of freeholders. What was happening in Chicago was happening everywhere industrialization and urbanization were taking place; but the sheer speed of the Midwestern metropolis' development and the determination with which it was declaring itself to be free from tradition were far from commonplace. Chicago in the years around the turn of the century was in many ways a microcosm of American society, and understanding the city as it appeared then is essential to comprehending the forces that changed the face of the country—and continue to change it to this day.

Contemporary writers, perhaps more than anybody else, understood the importance of the city, but, as literary critic Carl S. Smith has pointed out, "Chicago's growth was so rapid that the new city seemed foreign even to those writers who spent a great deal [...] of their intellectual and emotional substance in Chicago" (3). In their work as observers and organizers of the new city's facts, they constructed as many cities of feeling as they wrote books, and the result is, critic John T. Flanagan has argued with Dybek, that "[n]o major American city, not even New York, has figured more significantly, more memorably, in serious American fiction" (1966, 131). Chicago might have been the nation's second city in terms of population, but in literature, as well as in symbolic impact on American society, it was second to none. New Chicago phenomena, such as the seemingly uncontrolled industrialism, the appearance of the businessman as cultural hero, the developing middle class, and the inevitable slums accompanying large-scale urban development, naturally elicited a variety of different responses from writers trying to distill meaning from their rapidly changing environment. Writers such as Henry B. Fuller and Robert Herrick, dissatisfied with what they perceived as Chicago's culturally barren environment, attempted through a variety of literary strategies to create a place for literature in the city—and to put the city into literature. They gave birth to the modern American city novel about business and the art of making money, while other writers offered their own and remarkably different perspectives of the city. The popular newspaper column was invented in Chicago, and while the humorous sketches were originally meant as light entertainment, columnists such as Eugene Field and George Ade nevertheless produced literature of lasting quality that tells us much about the preoccupations of the growing Chicago middle class of clerks and shop girls. A third literary development was aimed at reforming social conditions. With rapid urban and industrial development, Chicago was home to perhaps the nation's most splendid display of material grandeur, but also to slums of abominable character. In the work of Jane Addams, Upton Sinclair and Jack London, the living conditions of many of the city's poorest inhabitants were put on display before the nation and helped build popular support for needed social reform.

With the flowering of artistic activity in the 1910s and early 1920s known as the Chicago Renaissance, the city became the center—for the Midwest as well as America—for new ideas in life and in literature. H. L. Mencken, in typical fashion, declared it to be "[t]he most civilized city in America [...] It is American in every chitling [sic] and sparerib, and it is alive from snout to tail" (5). Writers such as Sherwood Anderson and Carl Sandburg, however, were members of a movement without a unified credo, and the Chicago Renaissance soon dispersed to the East and Europe. With the arrival of the Depression, the growth and optimism of the great city came to a grinding halt. Rediscovering the fallen city in its various neighborhoods, a new generation of writers—including Farrell and Richard Wright—inspired by the Chicago School of Sociology took to the streets, creating there a microcosmic literature with a focus on the city's failure to offer, as Donald Pizer has said about America as a whole, "an adequate context for the development of the felt life" (1993, 35). Only in 1953, with Saul Bellow's decidedly local though geographically expansive *The Adventures of Augie March*, does a post-Depression Chicago character transcend his environment, and the result is a surprisingly optimistic and forward-thinking novel.

With attention to how the individual writer has described and evaluated the Chicago experience—creating a city of feeling from the city of fact—this book is an exploration of various literary attempts to understand what can perhaps be called the *meaning* of Chicago—and of how the city appears as a definable and undeniably unique presence in the diverse literature produced about it in the period from 1893 to 1953. But before there was a Chicago literature—let alone a tradition—there was the city itself, and before that there was the prairie. In order to understand the phenomenon that is Chicago, therefore, it is necessary first to take a look at some of the changes in American society that made its existence possible, changes that had almost entirely taken place by the time the city burst into the international consciousness in 1893.

—2—
The Making of a
Metropolis, 1833–1893

From the Agrarian Dream to
the Age of Great Cities

On July 12, 1893, famed historian Frederick Jackson Turner addressed the American Historical Association in Chicago. His paper, entitled "The Significance of the Frontier in American History," sprang from a recent bulletin of the Superintendent of the Census for 1890, which concluded, Turner quoted, that "the unsettled area has been so broken into by isolated bodies of settlement that there can hardly be said to be a frontier line" (1). Thus a country that had hitherto defined itself largely by its colonization of a free land, with its almost unlimited possibilities for westward expansion, now had to confront the reality of its external borders being firmly and irrevocably established. No more "virgin land," as historian Henry Nash Smith has called it, existed to be explored and settled, and with Turner pronouncing the closure of the frontier, the collective national myth of the inexhaustible West was intellectually disbanded.[1]

That Turner should be presenting his influential paper in Chicago in the year of the city's highly successful World's Columbian Exposition, constructed to showcase and celebrate industrial and scientific progress, seems notably appropriate. Nothing symbolized the

---

[1] For the standard discussion on the significance of the mythical West in American culture and society, see Henry Nash Smith, *Virgin Land* (1950).

end of an era and the beginning of another quite like Chicago. A village of 350 inhabitants in 1833, its population had soared to 300,000 by 1870 and reached the one million mark in 1890. Such unprecedented urban development, coupled with the rapid industrialization of both the economy and the population, naturally encouraged careful examination of the direction taken by the country toward becoming a nation of cities. "[F]our centuries from the discovery of America," Turner argued, and "at the end of a hundred years of life under the Constitution, the frontier has gone, and with its going has closed the first period of American history" (38). In 1893, then, the United States had reached a defining moment in its short history. It was by now no longer possible to regard American society as consisting mainly of farmers and plantation owners, and as the new national reality emerged, exemplified by both the Turner thesis and the World's Columbian Exposition in Chicago, many found themselves asking, as historian Alan Trachtenberg has phrased it, whether "the America fashioned on the frontier [would] survive the cauldrons of the city" (15).

Beginning with J. Hector St. John de Crèvecœur's *Letters from an American Farmer* published in 1782, with its descriptions of farmers working the "precious soil" (24), the early intellectual tradition of the American republic was largely preoccupied with the exploration and subsequent cultivation of a pure and untouched continent.[2] Early conceptions of America as a garden abounded, often with religious overtones of the colonizers as a chosen people in a new Eden. Farming the wild land appeared to be the American destiny, and Crèvecœur, seeing a fundamental connection between the land and the newly-established democracy, insisted that the conversion of "[t]his formerly rude soil [...] into a pleasant farm [...] has established all our rights; on it is founded our rank, our freedom, our power as citizens, our importance as inhabitants of such a district"

---

2   While the idea of the untouched continent naturally does not hold true, European eyes were so relatively blind to the marks made by the natives that this vision nevertheless endured for centuries.

(25). The land, it seemed, offered settlers all the things the majority of Americans had left Europe to find, and as the sheer magnitude of the continent further rendered unnecessary the huddling together in great urban centers based on the European model, cities appeared to be not only redundant, but also un-American.

In a famous passage from his only book, *Notes on the State of Virginia* (1781–1782), Thomas Jefferson, the nation's third president, argued from a decidedly anti-urban point of view that "[t]he mobs of great cities add just so much to the support of pure government, as sores do to the strength of the human body" (165).[3] The success of the American democratic experiment, Jefferson believed, rested upon the willingness of society to devote itself to a pure agrarian ideal consisting of simple and virtuous freeholders, while at the same time denouncing Old World civilization with its decadent and corrupt cities overflowing with vice and crime. Fearing also the coming of the industrial revolution and consequent massive urbanization as he had seen it in Europe, Jefferson, himself a farmer, made it clear that he believed that "[t]hose who labor in the earth are the chosen people of God" (164–165), and hoped thereby to point out an alternative direction for the country to move in.

The development of the nation's cities, however, despite these various intellectual efforts, could not be halted, although growth came slowly at first. In 1800 the largest city in America was Philadelphia, numbering 70,000, followed by New York at 60,000, Boston at 25,000, and Charleston at 18,000, and it was not until 1820 that more than eight percent of Americans had their homes in cities. That same year, New York and Philadelphia had grown to more than 100,000 each, and in the following half-century the urban population increased by an astounding 1,300 percent, while the overall population rose a com-

---

3 It is interesting to note that Jefferson, when elected president in 1800, worked closely with the architects Benjamin Latrobe and Pierre Charles L'Enfant in planning the great new American capital, the latter of which modeled the federal city on Versailles, with its diagonal boulevards emanating from a center.

paratively meager 300 percent. The country, in 1870, counted fourteen cities over 100,000, seven of which lay along the first transcontinental railroad, completed in 1869. Meanwhile, New York (including the city of Brooklyn, which was not officially annexed until 1898) had reached the one million mark.[4] Finally, and perhaps most strikingly, historian Arthur Schlesinger has noted that "[i]n the century from 1790 to 1890 the total population had grown 16-fold, while the urban segment grew 139-fold" (225). A country that had from its inception aspired to the ideal of a purely agrarian society was experiencing the effects of industrialism and was fast becoming urbanized. As cultural historian Leo Marx has observed, "[w]ithin the lifetime of a single generation, a rustic and in large part wild landscape was transformed into the site of the world's most productive industrial machine" (1964, 343).

This machine, of course, did not spring from nothing. The slightly delayed American version of the European Industrial Revolution of the late-eighteenth century, with its application of power-driven machinery to manufacturing, was instrumental in changing the face of the new republic. With it, masses of men, women and children took up factory work, and soon outnumbered people employed in the more traditional trades. Early factories operated mainly by water power and in rural areas, but with the invention and implementation of the steam engine around the turn of the century, industrial production was liberated from the streams of the countryside, and moved to the cities where cheap labor was more plentiful. Large urban centers in Western societies had hitherto been places of high culture, and of intellectual, political and scientific importance; but with the influx of large numbers of unskilled laborers and fortune-seekers, American city life was thoroughly transformed, and there emerged various new interpretations of the democratic principles formerly tied to the ownership and farming of land. Unprecedented levels of immigration, greatly affecting the ethnic and ideological composition of society, also appeared in the second half of the nineteenth century, along

4   All figures according to White (7), Siegel (3–4), and Bender (8).

with modern phenomena such as suburbs, slums and mass transit. These were the years, as historian Kenneth S. Lynn has summarized, when "the rate of industrialization and urbanization, the degree of social mobility, the absence of state control, the power of individuals, reached levels never before attained in American society" (9).

With urbanization and its consequences becoming impossible to ignore, a need and desire to comprehend and evaluate the changing realities appeared. Both Jefferson and Crèvecœur later realized the necessity of cities to the American experience and, as historian Thomas Bender has noted, "by mid-century, and especially after the Civil War, social thinkers realized that cities lay at the heart of American politics and society" (13).[5] Like Jefferson, Ralph Waldo Emerson believed that with a democracy founded on the appreciation of nature and the farming of land, America would increasingly disassociate itself from the artificial, corrupt and obsolete urbanity of Europe, and construct a new pastoral community. However, he argued late in life that "the test of civilization is the power of drawing the most benefits out of cities" (1914, 54).[6] The age of great cities had arrived, and for the public and intellectuals alike there could be no looking back.

---

5   In their influential but heavily criticized study of anti-urban sentiment in American thought *The Intellectual versus the City* (1962), Morton and Lucia White contend that an attitude of "ambivalence and animosity toward the city" has informed and dominated intellectual debate since the forming of the republic (1). Adrienne Siegel, in *The Image of the American City in Popular Literature, 1820–1870* (1981), seemingly written partly as a reply to the Whites' book, argues that while this tendency indeed existed among the "alienated intellectual elite," writers of popular fiction during the period in question, on the contrary "whetted the appetite of Americans for city life" (5). For a concise counterpoint to the Whites' book, and an enlightening discussion of many of the same themes, see Marx, "The Puzzle of Anti-Urbanism in Classic American Literature" (1981).

6   Emerson was, during a lifetime of writing, puzzlingly ambivalent on the question of cities. In 1844, for example, he had stated that "[c]ities give not the human senses room enough" (2007, 106) and that "[t]he city would have died out, rotted, and exploded, long ago, but that it was reinforced from the fields" (79). For a related discussion, see Cowan.

In the new version of America, as literary historian Malcolm Bradbury has perceptively theorized, two dominant movements thus emerged in society: "[T]he westering motion to the frontier, and the urbanizing motion toward the modern metropolis" (1993, 2). At the meeting point of these two great motions was the city of Chicago and its extraordinary growth from antebellum village to bustling megapolis in less than fifty years.

Years of Wonder
The Rise of Chicago

Chicago was first incorporated as a town in August 1833.[7] French explorers had visited the region in the seventeenth and eighteenth centuries, but no one found the low and swampy area sufficiently conducive to permanent settlement. Attracted mainly by the Chicago Portage, connecting Lake Michigan (or Lac des Illinois, as it was then known) with the Chicago River, and in turn allowing travelers into the Des Plaines River, the Illinois River, and finally the Mississippi, from where it was possible to reach the Mexican Gulf, these early explorers used the site mainly as an entry point for further exploration into the heart of the continent.

Generally considered to be the first permanent settler in what was to become Chicago, Jean Baptiste Point du Sable established a trading post there near the end of the eighteenth century, operating and expanding upon it for almost twenty years.[8] The establishment of Fort Dearborn at the site in 1803 angered native Americans, the

---

7   There is some confusion about the specific date of this event. The Chicago Public Library, for example, lists both August 5 and 12 as the day of the incorporation on their website.

8   Du Sable, an educated mulatto, remains a figure of some mystery, but it is generally believed that he was either a runaway slave, a native of Santo Domingo or Haiti, or a combination of both. William Cronon, however, identifies him as being from Quebec (26).

Potawatomis, and the inhabitants were killed in the famous massacre of 1812, rendering the area unstable until the reestablishment of the fort in 1816. This time the military held on, turning the fort into a valuable center for regional trade, and with the arrival of other settlers a small village was soon established. It was not until 1833, however, with the signing of several treaties forcing the Potawatomis off the land and further west, that the town reached some form of stability and could begin to make plans for the future.

The home to some 350 people, the town soon began to realize the strategic importance of its location.[9] With the completion of the Erie Canal in 1825, New York was finally connected, via the Hudson River and 363 miles of man-made waterways from Albany to Buffalo, with the Great Lakes, and along with them the emerging seaports of Milwaukee and Chicago, of which the latter, especially, attracted the attention of Eastern speculators. If the Chicago Portage could be substituted with a canal such as had been built in the East, large-scale inland transportation from New York all the way to New Orleans at the mouth of the Mississippi would be possible. This, in turn, would open up immense tracts of land along the way to Eastern development and exploitation. The resulting interest in Chicago real estate was enormous. Historian William Cronon writes that "[t]he mid-1830s saw the most intense land speculation in American history, with Chicago at the center of the vortex" (29), and that city lots "sold for $33 in 1829 were going for $100,000 by 1836" (29). Chicago was, at least in theory, the next big thing, and with the population passing 4,000 in 1837, the year after canal construction had begun, the town became a city and was incorporated as such on March 4. With no canal as yet, however, the aforementioned real estate prices represented nothing more than the speculators' great hopes for the future, and with actual construction on the ambitious project taking longer and proving more difficult than expected, the bubble burst, and the late

9 With no official numbers for the size of the population existing before 1840, this is an often-repeated estimate. All subsequent figures are according to the U.S. Census.

1930s and early 1940s witnessed the city's rapid early development reaching a standstill.

It was not until 1848 that the Illinois and Michigan Canal Corridor finally opened, and speculators could again begin to dream of the gigantic profits to be made in the process of Chicago becoming the center of trade for the new Midwest. The canal proved a successful investment, and during the first year of operation it facilitated an increase in eastern shipments of corn by an astounding 800 percent, as farmers found an alternative market to St. Louis (Cronon, 64). That same year, however, construction on the city's first railroad, the Galena and Chicago Union, had begun, an event that would become even more emblematic for the meteoric development of the city from frontier trading post to regional commercial center. Adapting the words of poet and dramatist John Jay Chapman, literary critic Alfred Kazin has famously noted that "the whole history of America after the Civil War was the story of a railroad passing through a town, and then dominating it" (1942, 19). In 1848 Chicago was already a city of 30,000, and the entrepreneurial domination had begun.

By 1840 the nation had a network of 2,818 miles of railroads in operation, a number that increased to 30,626 by the Civil War and to an extraordinary 166,703 miles by 1890 (Pursell, 78). The expansion of the railroad became the phenomenon of the age, and nowhere was it more instrumental to the success of a city than in Chicago. While its waterways and lakeside position were proving highly advantageous to directing farm produce from along the rivers away from St. Louis and into Chicago, the enormous hinterlands west of the Mississippi were not affected, and for that reason sparsely settled, until the large-scale implementation of railroads in the 1850s, with Illinois alone gaining around 2,500 miles of track by 1860 (Cronon, 68). The dominance of Chicago as a railroad center is perhaps best exemplified by the fact that all railroads reaching the city from the East terminated there, while all roads going further west had their starting point in Chicago. Floyd Dell, a writer associated with the Chicago Renaissance of the 1910s and early 1920s, describes in *Moon-Calf*, his autobiographical novel about the intellectual awakening of small-town boy Felix Fay, how his hero notices a map on the wall "in which a dozen iron roads were shown crossing the Middle West and centering in a dark blotch up in the corner" (393). That dark blotch was Chicago, which by the 1870s was the terminus of at least thirty different railroads. What was good for the railroad was good for Chicago, and so great was the power of the railroad companies that they were eventually allowed to build rails along the waterfront, separating the city from the lake by a wide band of tracks.[10]

With the farm produce of almost the entire country west of Chicago and north of St. Louis pouring in, and with trains reaching the Pacific in 1869, linking to the trade of the Orient, the city virtually exploded, necessitating the construction of such institutions and machinery as the Board of Trade and the Union Stock Yards.[11] When the population reached 110,000 in 1860, and almost tripled that number in the following decade, growth seemed unstoppable. The combination of Eastern interests and Western opportunity, as historian Everett Chamberlin and several others have noted, had formed the continent's first great inland metropolis, and it was not until Mrs. O'Leary's Cow, according to persistent local legend, tripped over a lantern and started what was to be known as the Great Fire of 1871 that the city experienced its first major setback.[12]

---

10 The introduction of standardized time zones bears testimony to the power of the railroads extending well beyond the realm of the physical world. In 1883, due to scheduling difficulties caused by the hundreds of local times existing in North America—by which the time in each town or city was set according to the position of the sun—the major railroad companies imposed the four time zones still in use today. It was not until 1918, however, that the U.S. Government officially acknowledged the change. For further discussion, see Pursell, *The Machine in America* (1995), 82, and Cronon, *Nature's Metropolis* (1991), 79.

11 1869 was also the year of the opening of the Suez Canal, further increasing the speed with which remote parts of the world could be reached. The Chicago Board of Trade was established by 82 local merchants in 1848 in order to centralize the buying and selling of grain. The Union Stock Yards opened on Christmas Day 1865.

12 See Everett Chamberlin, *Chicago and its Suburbs* (1874), 171–172. See

As if to fulfill Nathaniel Hawthorne's assertion in *The Marble Faun* eleven years earlier that "[a]ll towns should be made capable of purification by fire, or of decay within each half-century" (301), most of Chicago's downtown succumbed to flames on October 8–9, 1871. Approximately three hundred people lost their lives; one hundred thousand were left homeless; and property worth $190 million was destroyed, including 17,450 buildings in an area four miles long and almost a mile wide.[13] The preceding summer and early fall had seen the worst drought in decades, and Chicago, which consisted mainly of wooden buildings, had been rendered defenseless against the flames. The enterprising spirit that had characterized the city's quick growth, however, soon found its way back, and it was not long before people turned the conflagration into an opportunity to start anew, with better city planning—deciding this time to build in stone. True to booster form, the myth of the Phoenix miraculously rising from its own ashes was soon applied as a symbol of the unquenchable strength of Chicago and its will to regain its former greatness. Actually, little of the city's infrastructure had been damaged, and with a great influx of architects and engineers from the East, who realized the rare opportunity which presented itself to help reconstruct a great metropolis, the city was soon rebuilt.[14]

With business returning to normal, the population continued its steep curve upward and reached 500,000 in 1880, before finally breaking the one million mark in 1890. This made it the nation's second city, and boosters predicted that overtaking even New York would be merely a matter of time. The Chicago invention of the skyscraper soon dominated the scene, as if to make material the city's symbolic

---

also Anselm Strauss, *Images of the American City* (1961), 37, and Donald L. Miller, *City of the Century* (1997), 120, both of which discuss Chamberlin in detail.

13   Miller, 159 and Cronon, 345.

14   For a thorough discussion of the architecture of this period, the so-called "Chicago School" and its connection with, and symbolic use of, larger themes present in society, see Hugh Dalziel Duncan's *Culture and Democracy* (1965), especially chapters 4–8.

reaching for the sky, and its industrial enterprises and compounded financial structures heralded the coming of a new age, with business as the national vocation. The rise of capitalism naturally bred economic inequality, and consequently these were also the years of great social upheaval in the form of strikes, lockouts and civil unrest. Perhaps most infamous of all was the 1886 Haymarket Square bombing and subsequent trial, which many believed to be a mockery of justice as seven supposed anarchists were sentenced to death and another to fifteen years in prison.[15] Socialism, too, was beginning to gain a foothold in America as a result of increased immigration from Europe, and Chicago, with its enormous working class, was a natural center for the movement. This was not least because of the large number of Germans living in the city, an ethnic group never constituting less than twenty-five percent of the population between 1840 and the First World War.[16]

In the years following the fire Chicago had truly become more than the gateway city of its first incarnation, and was by now also a destination in itself. Arriving were both, as literary historian Marcus Cunliffe has called it, "[a] helpless immigrant proletariat" (220) and thousands of Midwestern farmers who thought not of New York, Boston, Paris or London when they dreamed big dreams of life in

---

15 The Haymarket bombing was an important event in American labor history. During an anarchist rally for the eight-hour working day, a bomb was suddenly thrown into the advancing police lines. Chaotic circumstances ensued, and when the smoke cleared seven police officers had been killed and sixty injured, more than half by friendly fire. The bomb-thrower was never found, and a direct connection between the bombing and the eight accused men was never established. In effect convicted solely for being anarchists, four of the seven who were sentenced to death were later executed or, as William Dean Howells called it in a letter to Hamlin Garland, "civically murdered" (1928, 407). A plethora of books exist about the Haymarket affair, but see Paul Avrich, *The Haymarket Tragedy* (1984) for an interesting account with the focus on the anarchists themselves, as well as their sometimes-militant struggle to reform society.

16 See Miller, 468–470, for a fuller account of the German minority's position in Chicago.

the city, but only of their own local prairie metropolis, the one that had sprung from the land around it and carried the sound of progress in the machine-like syllables of its very name.

The World's Columbian Exposition of 1893 was locally regarded as Chicago's fulfillment of its destiny. Only sixty years old and already the home of a million people, Chicago was about to enter, along with America herself, its second period. Time would tell if the sixty years to come would prove to be as prosperous as the previous sixty, but one thing was certain: the future had arrived, and Chicagoans were ready to conquer it.

Toward a Literary City
Hamlin Garland and Sherwood Anderson

The extraordinary shift in American society from the country to the city, both factually and imaginatively, has intrigued writers of fiction from the very beginning. In the case of Chicago, however, it took several decades before fiction about the city, and the experience it offered, began to appear, and when it did, its quality was sometimes negligible. Edward Bonney's exquisitely titled *The Banditti of the Prairies; or, the Murderer's Doom! A Tale of the Mississippi Valley* from 1850 is generally considered the first novel to emerge from the city, and it was shortly followed by an assortment of frontier-themed romances and adventure stories, penned mostly as pure entertainment for the ever-increasing population. It was not until 1872 and the publication of Edward Payson Roe's *Barriers Burned Away* that a "Chicago novel" could be said to exist. Literary historian Kenny J. Williams calls it "a sentimental work with the sensationalism of the Chicago Fire and the moralistic preachments of its central character" (1980, 248), and the book is certainly little more than an unabashed celebration of the city's astonishing rebirth after the fire. Overflowing with lofty statements such as calling Chicago "the greatest city in the world. Only the other day her streets were prairies" (376), the book is, however, an important precursor to many of the themes that would dominate the fiction of Chicago in the years around the turn of the century.[17] Its hero, Dennis Fleet, arrives in the city from a small town and quickly begins to make his way around the business district, making up a new set of values suitable to modern city life as he goes along. Chicago novels continued in this vein but without much artistic success, until the publication of Henry B. Fuller's *The Cliff-Dwellers* in 1893, which brought a critical voice and considerable artistic skill to many of the same themes.[18] It is notable that the central experience of Chicago during these years, the turning of a village into an industrial metropolis, did not find a place in its early literature. Perhaps it required the perspective of later years to comprehend and evaluate the passing of small-town agricultural Midwestern America, and the subsequent supremacy of the machines of capitalism. These themes later found their true chronicler with Sherwood Anderson in the 1910s and 1920s but, going one step further down the ladder of urban development, the literature of the country's transition—and the bridging of the gap between the two worlds—began in 1891, when Hamlin Garland was still an angry young man and published *Main-Travelled Roads*, his devastating account of the hardship endured by farmers on the Western frontier.

Garland was the son of a pioneering farmer who, in the years after the Civil War, took his family on a seemingly endless quest for better land and bigger profits, following the expanding Western frontier

---

17   The book, however, despite its obvious flaws, was a tremendous success. According to James D. Hart, "a 'limited' edition of a hundred thousand copies was immediately sold out" ten years after the original printing (121).

18   For a thorough exploration into the literatures of Chicago before 1893, see Kenny J. Williams, *Prairie Voices: A Literary History of Chicago from the Frontier to 1893* (1980). Williams has done an impressive job of procuring obscure texts from all fields of literature, and the result, especially when read as accompanying her massive *In the City of Men: Another Story of Chicago* (1974), is never less than interesting. The appendices, covering everything from an index of journals on agriculture to endless lists of publishers operating in Chicago before 1893, are amazingly complete and constitute an indispensable tool for further research.

through Wisconsin, Iowa and South Dakota. With vague aspirations of becoming a writer, Garland left the farm for Boston in 1884 and spent the next three years educating himself at the Boston Public Library, befriending William Dean Howells in the process. Upon returning home in 1887, he was alarmed by the poverty and isolation of his family and their neighbors. Remembering Joseph Kirkland's advice to him that he was "the first actual farmer in American fiction,—now tell the truth about it" (Garland 1995, 298), Garland vowed to put their story into fiction.[19] The resulting book, a collection of six short stories, or "sketches," dedicated "[t]o my father and mother whose half-century pilgrimage on the main-travelled road of life has brought them only toil and deprivation" was a bitter account of what Garland believed to be a betrayal of the agrarian dream.[20] "Go west, young man, and grow up with the country" had been the motto for generations of migrant farmers, but what they had found there was not an American Eden of fertile soil and soft hills, but a life of drudgery spent cultivating the wild land in an often harsh climate.[21]

While seldom artfully constructed, many of Garland's stories are nevertheless both interesting and surprisingly powerful as they recount the daily struggle to stay alive on what he called "the middle border." This is partly due to his fierce determination to tell the truth about rural decay, but also because they illustrate a fundamental change in the values of American society. As historians Brian Lee and Robert Reinders have pointed out, the public image of the farmer in the years after the Civil War moved from "the noble yeoman" to

---

19   Kirkland, a Chicago lawyer, was the author of *Zury: The Meanest Man in Spring County*, which had been published in New York earlier in 1887 and was the first Illinois novel to reach a national audience. Garland, never one to neglect an opportunity such as this, soon struck up a friendship with Kirkland.

20   Garland was a prolific writer who intermittently added new pieces to the various editions. The collection would eventually swell to eleven stories.

21   The motto is generally ascribed to Horace Greeley, owner of the New York *Tribune* and one of the founders of the Republican Party, but John L. Soule in the Terre Haute *Express* has also been claimed as the source.

that of "a 'hayseed', 'rube' or 'hick'" (185)—a comical figure of ridicule on the stages of urban vaudeville. The best of Garland's stories, "Up the Coolly," follows a character who has left the farm at an early age and made a name for himself as an actor in New York.[22] When he, much like Garland, visits home after several years in the city, he finds his brother, who stayed and worked the land, to be "a brute, a fool!" (86). The first meeting between the two illustrates perfectly just how irreconcilable the divide has become:

> They stood and looked at each other. Howard's cuffs, collar, and shirt, alien in their elegance, showed through the dusk, and a glint of light shot out from the jewel of his necktie, as the light from the house caught it at the right angle. As they gazed in silence at each other, Howard divined something of the hard, bitter feeling which came into Grant's heart as he stood there, ragged, ankle-deep in muck, his sleeves rolled up, a shapeless old straw hat on his head (79).

Howard—and American society in thought and fact—had moved on from the country and toward the city, but had left behind in the process, struggling in the "muck," a helpless class of crude farmers for whom the opportunities offered by the city would definitively remain out of reach.

After the wretched inhabitants of the raw prairie, the next stage in Midwestern development toward the city was the small town, and one of its finest storytellers is Sherwood Anderson. Anderson was born in a small town in Ohio in 1876. His early life was spent attending school and working various jobs, from newsboy to stable hand, preparing for a life as a small-scale businessman. He soon established himself as president of a mail-order paint company in Elyria,

---

22   A "coolly" is a broad and shallow valley typical of the Northwest of Garland's youth. The word comes from the French *coulée*, and Garland seems to be in some confusion about which form to use—often using both interchangeably within the same story or, later in his career, novel.

Ohio, later renamed the Anderson Manufacturing Company, where he sold a roof-extending paint called "Roof-Fix." Anderson was dissatisfied with the mercantile nature of his small-town existence, and he dabbled in writing poems and short stories in his spare time. Shortly after suffering a nervous breakdown in 1912, he left his wife and three children and moved to Chicago, where he soon became associated with the booming literary scene while making his living writing advertising copy.[23] Always drawing largely on his own life and experiences for material, Anderson's dissatisfaction with small-town life naturally found an outlet in literature, and his first major success, *Winesburg, Ohio*, was therefore intended to expose the dying American small town and its increasing inability to satisfy the mental lives of its inhabitants. Composed of a series of interrelated short stories, each concerned with a citizen of the town, the book describes a stultifying and spiritually barren environment and illuminates the frustrations and long-suppressed desires of the townspeople in the process. The central character, George Willard, is a somewhat naïve young reporter for the *Winesburg Eagle*, and the novel finds its climax in his final decision to leave Winesburg and go to Chicago, "as if," Malcolm Bradbury has pointedly noted, "the quest for self and art alike can only be carried out in the glare and existential exposure of the city" (1991, 101). As the train is about to leave, George falls into a daze of contemplation, and when he again looks out the

---

23   Anderson himself had, in his three autobiographical volumes, a tendency to romanticize many aspects of his life. In *A Story Teller's Story*, for example, he portrays his early writing of stories as a secret best kept from his business associates in Elyria, while in reality, David D. Anderson maintains, it was "almost common knowledge" (1967, 14). Similarly, he never mentioned his breakdown but preferred to mythologize that his break with business had occurred when, in the middle of dictating a letter to his secretary, he was suddenly overwhelmed with disgust for his commercial life and, looking at his feet, said to the confused secretary: "My feet are cold, wet, and heavy from long wading in a river. Now I shall go walk on dry land," after which he walked along the railroad tracks out of town, resolving on the way to dedicate the rest of his life to literature (1924, 496).

window, "the town of Winesburg had disappeared and his life there had become but a background on which to paint the dreams of his manhood" (153). Much like Anderson himself, George has to go to Chicago to escape the slow suffocation of rural town life, and, with their mutual breaking away, another phase of Midwestern urbanization had been left behind.[24]

After the intensely personal and almost cathartic experience of writing *Winesburg, Ohio*, Anderson nevertheless felt that the subject matter—this being 1919—was already of a somewhat antiquated character. In a letter to Van Wyck Brooks, whom he had recently met in New York, he wrote about his recognition of the changing face of America:

> One has to realize that, although there is truth in the Winesburg things, there is another big story to be done. We are no longer the old America. Those are tales of farming people. We've got a new people now. We are a growing, shifting, changing thing. Our life in our factory towns intensifies. It becomes at the same time more ugly and more intense" (*Letters*, 31).

The result of these contemplations was the novel *Poor White*, an ambitious account of the rapid industrialization of a small Midwestern town, published in 1920.

---

24   *Winesburg, Ohio* shares many characteristics and its major theme with Edgar Lee Masters's *The Spoon River Anthology*, a monumental collection of 246 free-verse poems published in 1915 to great acclaim. The poems, all relatively short, are each narrated from the cemetery by a deceased citizen of Spoon River, Illinois, voicing many of the same complaints about the frustrations and limitations of small-town life as the citizens of Winesburg. The chief accomplishment of the book, however, is in its inventive way of giving each poem a distinctive voice and point of view, telling the same stories many times, but within different contexts. Masters, a prosperous Chicago lawyer, published the book under pseudonym, fearing for his law practice should the public find out that he had spent his time writing poetry. A second volume of epitaphs, the less successful *The New Spoon River*, appeared in 1924.

As the novel opens, the town of Bidwell, Ohio, is a small and rural nineteenth-century trading center, not unlike Winesburg, populated by farmers, craftsmen and shopkeepers. With the arrival in town of "horse-like" (271) Hugh McVey, however, a "Huckleberry Finn turned Henry Ford" (David D. Anderson 1995, 18), the boom comes to Bidwell and the Jeffersonian world of the town and its surrounding country soon becomes a thing of the past. Moving to Bidwell from a lazy river town in Missouri, Hugh is an isolated and socially inept young man who takes a job in the railroad-office outside town, where he secretly, and mostly for his own pleasure, invents machinery to facilitate various tasks which he sees the townspeople performing manually. As expected, this industrial revolution incarnate and his inventions are discovered by an enterprising man from town, and before long, as "the giant, Industry" (131) awakes, deals are made, money is invested, factories are built and workers are being recruited from among the farmhands. The country is changing, Anderson writes, rather heavy-handedly, and the people are changing with it:

> Boys, who in the schools had read of Lincoln, walking for miles through the forest to borrow his first book [...] began to read in the newspapers and magazines of men who by developing their faculty for getting and keeping money had become suddenly and overwhelmingly rich. Hired writers called the men great, and there was no maturity of mind in the people with which to combat the force of the statement, often repeated (131).

The gospel of the industrial machine thus replaces traditional values, and the cunning yet intellectually helpless citizens, who before the boom were relatively equal in social and economic standing, establish, as literary critic Blanche Housman Gelfant has commented, "new relationships of inequality, of capitalist and worker, employer and employee" (102). Anderson himself, in *A Story Teller's Story*—his first volume of autobiography—despondently concluded about the industrialized mind that these were the years in which "[d]reams [...] were to be expressed in building railroads and factories, in boring gas wells, stringing telegraph poles. There was room for no other dream" (26).

Sherwood Anderson was ambivalent in his literary treatment of small-town America. Where in *Winesburg, Ohio* he deplored the staleness of the lives lived there, in *Poor White* he took the opposite stand and celebrated the delicacy and sweetness of the nation's rural areas as they existed before the industrial revolution. True, he concluded, the urbanization of America offered great freedom and an abundance of opportunities for the creative mind, but if the nation did not tread carefully into the new industrial age, it would someday wake up to realize, along with Hugh near the end of *Poor White*—and in typical Anderson fashion—that "[t]he gods have thrown the towns like stones over the flat country, but the stones have no color. They do not burn in the light" (358). The Midwestern community that started life as the prairie farms of Hamlin Garland's *Main-Travelled Roads* had evolved first into Winesburg, then experienced the process of industrialization along with Bidwell, and was on its way to becoming another gray and colorless city. No city, of course, in Anderson's imaginary, was grayer or more colorless than Chicago, and the city had proved to be, for the Midwest and its literature alike, a present-day incarnation of the country's future.

Uncharted Literature
Chicago and the Literary West

As Midwestern authors in the early 1890s increasingly turned to Chicago for material, they found a landscape largely foreign to literature. Little had been written about the city or, for that matter, almost any city in America. Classical American literature had, due mostly to the nation's frontier history, largely centered around man's encounter with nature in one form or another, or had been imitative of European styles and forms. Chicago, on the other hand, as Robert Herrick, one of the city's early chroniclers wrote in *The Gospel of Freedom*, was "an instance of successful, contemptuous disregard of nature by man" (101). And, as if to make matters even worse, it was not, as the American East, modeled on European urban experience, but had sprung independently from the swamp on which it stood, suited only to the one task it was built to perform: the buying and selling of various commodities.

The problem of putting the relatively novel concept of the industrial city into literature was not quite a new one. The Romantic poets of late-eighteenth and early-nineteenth-century England were among the first to encounter this difficulty. At a time when Americans generally still believed in Jefferson's ideal rural society, the native country of the Romantic poets was changing and, instead of changing with it, they opted for, as literary historian Stephen Spender has argued about their writing, "total rejection of the modern city" (46). The phrase "total rejection," however, is a bit too categorical, and certainly to Wordsworth, in "Composed upon Westminster Bridge, September 3, 1802," London could be both beautiful and worthy of poetic mention in the earliest morning hours, when it most resembled—and almost became part of—nature, as it lay "[o]pen unto the fields, and to the sky," and when the daytime clamor of the industrial city could almost be forgotten because "the very houses seem[ed] asleep" (296). The Romantic movement, seen in light of contemporary society, Spender further argues, can be construed as "an immense rearguard action [...] [leaving] poetry with a vocabulary capable of dealing only with the poet in some Romantic situation" (46), and the difficult but inevitable task of finding a place for the modern city in literature was left to later generations. Charles Dickens, writing most prolifically at mid-century, is often credited with inventing the modern city for literary purposes. In *Bleak House*, for example, the London fog carries profound metaphorical significance, and the investment of phenomena specific to an urban environment with complexities of meaning previously not found in city literature was an important development. Literary critic Irving Howe has argued that it is in Dickens, along with Nikolai Gogol in Russia, that "[t]he modern city first appears full-face—as physical concreteness, emblem of excitement, social specter, and locus of myth" (42). He concludes later in the same essay that with its appearance as a "major locale[,] [...] [l]iterature gains a new freedom; everything, which may be too much, is now possible" (48).

In Chicago in the 1890s, too much—or perhaps too little—was certainly possible. The old cities of Europe and its American imitations along the East Coast all existed for things other than the making of money, and could additionally draw upon history and tradition, even if only in small measures, in their search for contemporary literary expression. The world of old and established London and, to a lesser degree, New York society offered the novels of Henry James and Edith Wharton a congenial environment; but, in comparison, what historian Asa Briggs has called the "shock city" (51) of Chicago was a new and unprecedented experience. Here was no London fog, and the rising skyscrapers and grid-pattern street layout reminded one not of nature but of artifice in the extreme. The city never slowed down long enough to be perceived as peaceful, and an established society so important to literary Europe and what George Santayana later called the genteel tradition of the American East was nowhere in sight.[25] Here, on the other hand, was something at the same time typically American and uniquely Western, and it was little wonder that when the call finally came for a local literature, what was asked of writers was to create something new and exciting, something that would capture the energy of the city and the variety of its people—a literature born of the West. What that would entail, exactly, and in what measures, became the subject of discussion in the first journals and literary circles of the city, where writers such as Hamlin Garland—who had moved to Chicago from Boston in the hope of finding a group of writers to lead and inspire—began to debate the issues with others who shared their interest in developing a distinct Western literature.

---

25 Santayana argued that a division existed in America between "aggressive enterprise" and "genteel tradition," and also noted, in a passage seemingly suggested by Chicago, that "[t]he American Will inhabits the sky-scraper; the American Intellect inhabits the colonial mansion" (188).

On October 1, 1893, during the closing days of the World's Columbian Exposition, the *Dial* of Chicago, a rather conservative paper, published an editorial entitled "The Literary West." The editorial expressed dismay over the condescending attitude of Eastern critics toward the West, which, it was felt, promoted the success of loud but undeserving Western writers, vulgarizing in the process the entire concept of Western literature:

> When an Eastern writer undertakes to discuss the literary activities of the West, he almost invariably falls into the error of the foreign critic, and singles out as noteworthy and typical the writers whose work evinces some sort of eccentricity. It may be badly written, it may be grotesque, it may be vulgar—it frequently has all three of these characteristics,—but it is original, it is piquant, it satisfies the unholy yearning for the new thing. Some composer of dialect doggerel, cheaply pathetic or sentimental, gains the ear of the public; his work has nothing more than novelty to recommend it, but the advent of a new poet is heralded, and we are told by Eastern critics that the West has at least found a voice. Some strong-lunged but untrained product of the prairies recounts the monotonous routine of life on the farm or in the country town, and is straightway hailed as the apostle of the newest and consequently the best realism (174).

With its insistence that whatever is Western need not be wild, the article argued that a distinction between Eastern and Western literature in terms of style was meaningless since, after all, "[t]he West and the East are peopled by the same sort of men and women, […] [and] many of the best writers from either section came to it from the other" (175). Concluding that "[t]he coming literature of the West may be largely Western in its themes, but it will never be Western in its manner" (175), the editorial encouraged equal treatment based on a common set of aesthetic values for literary activity within the nation, while at the same time recognizing that a certain difference of themes and subject matter would naturally evolve in the different regions as writers typically respond to their immediate environment.

The article's unmasked attack on Hamlin Garland and his followers, however, did not discourage Garland from seeking his literary fortune in Chicago. He had started his crusade for a Western literature with *Main-Travelled Roads* in 1891, and with its success had become, especially to Eastern critics, the insufferable "voice of the West" mentioned in the *Dial's* editorial. Unaffected by such criticism, however, Garland based himself in Chicago, seeing the city as the natural center for the movement, and published *Crumbling Idols* in 1894, a book of criticism that he considered to be his Declaration of Independence for Western literature. Furthermore, as if to prove that the West had freed itself from the East in all respects, Garland let the small but ambitious Chicago firm Stone and Kimball publish the book, although *Main-Travelled Roads* had been published by the prestigious and influential Arena Publishing Company in Boston.[26]

The revolution thus launched in spirit and body, Garland argued strongly in the book for "the revolt against the domination of the East" (119) which, he said, was no longer American. Ralph Waldo Emerson had argued in 1857, in *The American Scholar*, that the nation's "long apprenticeship to the learning of other lands" was drawing to a close (525). Now the time had come, Garland insisted, for the West to shed all Eastern influence and create a literature where "life is the model and truth the criterion" (120). For the book Garland coined the term "veritism," which functioned as a middle ground between the mild and rather bloodless realism of his friend William Dean Howells and the bleak naturalism of Emile Zola.[27] To this Garland added a

---

26   For an analysis of Garland's motives in changing his publisher, as well as several letters by Garland to Stone and Kimball, see John T. Flanagan, "Hamlin Garland Writes to his Chicago Publisher" (1952).

27   For a discussion of the influence upon Garland's ideas of French philosopher Eugene Véron—from whose name he possibly derived the term "veritism"—see Donald Pizer, *Realism and Naturalism in Nineteenth-Century American Literature* (1976), chapter 8.

strong preference for localism and concluded: "This is, I believe, the essence of veritism: 'Write of those things of which you know most, and for which you care most. By so doing you will be true to yourself, true to your locality, and true to your time'" (30). Indeed, he believed the local novel to be "the most promising of all literary attempts to-day; certainly it is the most sincere" (59). Western writers, according to Garland, should cease to imitate the East, and instead seek out local material, of which they could write intuitively and truthfully, and by doing so they would create, almost by default, a fundamentally independent literature filled with the vitality of the West.

Garland, however, did not settle for presenting his ideas in a book of literary theory that he knew few would read, and consequently he explored many of the same ideas in his novel *Rose of Dutcher's Coolly*, which was published in 1895, the year after *Crumbling Idols*. Rose is a Wisconsin farm girl whose capacities for beauty and art are awakened when she attends a circus performance in a nearby town. Her idealized infatuation with one of the stars of the show, the heroic William de Lisle, lasts for years and acts as a constant reminder to her that there is indeed a world beyond her Wisconsin coolly. Rose makes her way first to Madison in order to attend college, and later to Chicago, and because of her wholesome appearance and decidedly artless disposition, she is considered by many to be a sort of natural prodigy who will find great success in the city. Her literary output, however, is "an echo of Tennyson" (241) and, in the words of Garland's narrative voice, reflects "all the conventional positions in literature. She stood upon the graves of the dead as if she feared they might be desecrated" (220). Defending "Emerson and Thoreau as if she were [...] [an] easterner" (218), Rose nevertheless needs only a little guidance from Warren Mason, the city's preeminent literary critic—and a character clearly modeled on Garland himself—before she can let her true Western voice out. Melodramatically compelling her to burn her old manuscripts after attending a concert in the city's famous and acoustically perfect Auditorium Theatre, Mason introduces her to what he believes to be themes suited for the new literature: "See these lovers walking before and behind us. He may be a clerk in a bank; she the banker's daughter. That man Harvey, in whose box you sit tonight, was a farmer's boy, and his wife the daughter of a Methodist preacher in a cross-roads town. How did they get where they are, rich, influential, kindly, polished in manner? What an epic!" (276).[28] Rose, in this way, soon comes to understand the value of a new Western and democratic literature, and where she had previously spent her days on the farm dreaming of William de Lisle, she now, upon returning for a visit, finds "every familiar thing [...] [to have] taken on a peculiar value—a literary and artistic value" and discovers that "[a] red barn set against a gray-green wooded hillside was no longer commonplace. 'How pretty!' she thought; 'I never noticed that before'" (371). As seen through the prism of veritism, Rose learns, there is beauty and truth to be found in everything previously considered ordinary, but the determination with which this point is made ultimately, and unfortunately, makes her less a convincing character than a fictionalized embodiment of Garland's theories.

The battle over Western literature thus raging, it is important to notice that the editorial in the *Dial* and Garland agreed upon at least one thing. There could be no doubt that Chicago and the West were indeed fit subjects for literature, and that the newness of the region would challenge its writers to find appropriate ways to deal with the themes and subject matter offered, however foreign to literature they might seem. In the case of Chicago, the city represented to most people a mixture of the modern, the industrial, and the material, and was thus emblematic of forces appearing in society as a whole. Yet no

---

28   It is ironic that Mason, or Garland, should be making this observation immediately after a concert of Richard Wagner described as "glorious beyond words" in the Auditorium (275). The Western revolution, apparently, did not extend into the realm of music. The interest in the lives of successful people also in a small way anticipates what Larzer Ziff has called "the domestication of Hamlin Garland" (103) and what Garland's friend Henry B. Fuller satirized in the *roman à clef* "The Downfall of Abner Joyce," the first story in *Under the Skylights*. See the present chapter on Fuller for further discussion of this and other themes.

literature adequately interested in these themes existed, and the use of urban settings had, until then, predominantly been employed to accommodate society novels in New York or Boston.[29] The incorporation of these ungainly concepts into literature was not an easy task, and writers such as Emerson, according to literary critic Michael H. Cowan, "believed that the 'test or measure of poetic genius' was its ability to transform the circumstances 'of the nineteenth century' into literary material [...] [and] 'to convert the vivid energies acting at this hour in New York and Chicago and San Francisco into universal symbols'" (3–4). Nowhere, of course, were these vivid energies more visible than in Chicago, and in the forms of the railroad, the skyscraper, the slums and the stockyards, the city seemed to consist mostly of things impossible to describe in traditional and conventional language. In this spirit, British journalist George Warrington Steevens, reporting for the London *Daily Mail*, wrote home in 1896: "Not if I had a hundred tongues, every one shouting a different language in a different key, could I do justice to her splendid chaos" (144). He was echoed some years later by American travel writer Julian Street who, despairingly, said: "Call Chicago mighty, monstrous, multifarious, vital, lusty, stupendous, indomitable, intense, unnatural, aspiring, puissant, preposterous, transcendent—call it what you like—throw the dictionary at it!" (139). With inherited forms, of society as well as literature, thus having little relevance amid the glaring newness and "splendid chaos" of their city, writers found themselves with an almost blank slate and, perhaps more importantly, a new set of realities out

---

29   To be fair, William Dean Howells's *The Rise of Silas Lapham* (1885) had chronicled the ascent of a Vermont farmer as he discovers a paint mine on his property and founds a successful business, but had done so in decidedly old-fashioned terms, insisting on the moral integrity of its central character. The early 1890s also saw the publication of such urban-themed novels as Howells's *A Hazard of New Fortunes* (1890) and Stephen Crane's *Maggie: A Girl of the Streets* (1893), both of which took place in New York and added new aspects to the urban literary experience. But the new age of ruthless big-city capitalism had yet to be recorded in literature.

of which to craft the literature of Chicago—realities exemplified in 1893 by the city's World's Columbian Exposition.

—3—
Writing Chicago, 1893–1923

The World's Columbian Exposition

With the World's Columbian Exposition in 1893, Chicago burst into the nation's consciousness and, many believed, fulfilled the promise it had spent sixty years making. Intended to commemorate the 400-year anniversary of the discovery of America, the Exposition arrived one year late, although the dedication ceremonies had been held in October 1892. The selection of Chicago as the location for the Fair had been controversial, and the city had overcome hard competition from New York, St. Louis and Washington, D.C., to host the event.[30] In the end, however, Chicago was chosen because it exemplified more than its competitors the modernity and diligence of the young nation, qualities valued highly at a fair dedicated to exhibiting recent developments in, as the official program put it, "arts, industries, manufactures, and the product of the soil, mine and sea" (quoted in Williams 1974, 145).

Daniel Burnham, the architect placed in charge of construction of the fairgrounds, envisioned a grandiose and classical "White City," after which the Exposition later gained its popular name, while another famous Chicago architect, Louis H. Sullivan, wished to use the opportunity to draw attention to American innovations in the arts,

---

30   For a detailed account of the political decision to hold the Fair in Chicago, as well as the architectural preparations, see Kenny J. Williams, *In the City of Men: Another Story of Chicago* (1974), chapter 4.

and especially those of Chicago.[31] After Burnham's plan had prevailed, however, Sullivan had to settle for designing the Transportation Building, which he made sure would stand out from the white buildings by Burnham and his associates by creating a polychromatic façade and an immense gilded entrance. The physical appearance of the Exposition was, when it finally opened early in 1893, a mass of classical buildings arranged around a European-style Court of Honor, and constructed in cheap materials intended to last only for the duration of the Fair. The challenge of the organizers had been to suggest that America had reached cultural equality with Europe, while at the same time indicating the distinctiveness of the American experience, a balance that, according to several visitors, had been completely missed. In *Amy Leslie at the Fair*, a collection of chatty letters relating to the Exposition and published in the same year, journalist Lillie West Brown Buck related how disappointed she was by "the endless procession of the tiresomely perfect gods and goddesses, allegories, revered freaks, and European celebrities" (17), preferring to have instead "a group of ungovernable prairie horses, startling western riders, and Daniel Boone, Kit Carson, old Jim Bridger or Wild Bill" (20). More recently, literary historian Larzer Ziff has described how especially visitors from Europe "[c]onvinced already of American commercial and technical superiority […] had come to Chicago to learn how this modern spirit was to embody itself in form, and […] found, instead, uninteresting imitations of the ruins of the Old World" (20). Outside the fairgrounds, in what condescending visitors called the "gray city," architectural history was being made as skyscrapers rose higher and higher almost on a daily basis, while inside the gates the West was again imitating Europe and the East, contributing, as Henry B. Fuller wrote, "nothing toward solving the problems that

---

31   That the name "White City" carries connotations of the Exposition not being racially inclusive has not escaped critical attention. For an enlightening discussion of this and other themes associated with the Fair, see Mary Esteve, *The Aesthetics and Politics of the Crowd in American Literature* (2003), chapter 4.

confront the modern architect" (1899, 223).[32] Too eager to show the world that Chicago was truly a magnificent city comparable with the best the world had to offer, and too eager to please the often classicist tastes of influential Eastern critics, the organizers had abandoned all ambition of reflecting American art and culture in the design of the fairgrounds, and the Exposition in this way became a clear parallel to the East-West controversy in literature.

Hamlin Garland, however, did not seem to mind. As he later recalled in the first of a long series of autobiographies, *A Son of the Middle Border* (1917), he was "Amazed at the grandeur" (367–368) of the Exposition and consequently wrote to his parents in South Dakota: "Sell the cook stove if necessary and come. You *must* see this fair" (368). Indeed the Exposition, despite its unimaginative exterior, contained much to see and admire. Determined to showcase the world of tomorrow, it consisted of over two hundred buildings which housed endless exhibitions of state-of-the-art industrial machinery and household electronics such as the telephone and the phonograph, as well as such unique items as the world's most powerful telescope, its largest cannon, and a model of the Liberty Bell made entirely of wheat, oats and rye. Immensely impressed with the spectacle of "The Magic City" (369), Garland forgot for the moment his theories of Western art among the belly dancers and fakirs, imported to entertain the more than 27 million people who visited the enormously popular Exposition.

The Fair, however, as a symbol of forces present in society at large, was equally exciting to a somewhat different visitor with a comparatively stronger analytical mind and an entirely different education. Always to be found at the center of things, Henry Adams also made the journey to Chicago in 1893, where he spent more time with the dynamos than with the belly dancers, in order that he might better

---

32 Perhaps commenting most vehemently, the embittered Sullivan, evaluating the artistic impact of the exposition on American architecture in *The Autobiography of an Idea* (1924), concluded famously that "[t]he damage wrought by the World's Fair will last for half a century from its date, if not longer" (325).

understand where his country was heading. Probably stopping on his way to admire the display of his grandfather John Quincy Adams's baby clothes, Adams made his way around the Exposition in a state of constant absorption, finding, as he wrote in his ironical third person autobiography, *The Education of Henry Adams*, all "matter of study there to fill a hundred years" (339). Finally sitting down to brood as he "had never brooded on the benches of Harvard College," Adams realized the helplessness of his historical mind before "a mechanical sequence" (342) and the futility of standing up for "his eighteenth century, his Constitution of 1789, his George Washington" (343) amidst the machinery of The Electricity Building and the commercial spirit that was the backbone of the entire enterprise.[33] "Chicago," Adams concluded, "asked in 1893 for the first time the question whether the American people knew where they were driving" (343). The country was rapidly changing, and the values on which it was founded had been left behind, exemplified in the official motto of the Exposition, which promised to "Make Culture Hum!"

The World's Columbian Exposition represented several things. One was the coming of age of Chicago, now a city of more than one million inhabitants, and second only to New York within the nation. Another was the city's grand ambition to be free in body and spirit from the influence of the East while ultimately remaining dependent upon the tastes and opinions of Eastern critics. But also, the Fair represented the symbolic power of Chicago, with its undisguised emphasis on industry and business, as a new moral and geographic center for an entire generation. The city was, Adams acknowledged, "the first expression of American thought as a unity; one must start

---

33   The professed purpose of the Fair was to showcase artistic and industrial developments for a public eager to be educated, but many visitors commented on the blatant commercialism permeating everything. Representatively, the novelist Edward Bellamy, best known for his utopian fantasies such as *Looking Backward, 2000 to 1887*, wrote: "The underlying motive of the whole exhibition, under a sham pretense of patriotism is business, advertising with a view to individual money-making" (quoted in Trachtenberg, 215).

there" (343). As Chicago became a center for the modern American imagination, all of these themes found their way into the literature that slowly began to incorporate such new elements as the Board of Trade and the accompanying industrial machine.

The Businessman, Art and Society in a City out of Control

The magnificence and opulence of the Chicago vision was exemplified by the World's Columbian Exposition, but it was perhaps the city itself that was the real attraction. Chicago was modern in the extreme, and being the birthplace of both the skyscraper and the elevated railroad, the look and sound of progress was everywhere. Always measuring success by the scale of its industrial and monetary achievements, the city was home to some of the nation's biggest business conglomerates, whose leaders were prominent figures in society.[34] Men such as Marshall Field, George Pullman and Potter Palmer led the procession of insatiable materialism into the twentieth century, accumulating massive fortunes along the way.[35] In Chicago lived the

---

34 Exemplary of the new scale on which things were done, the University of Chicago was founded in 1893 with a check for $2,600,000, given by John D. Rockefeller.

35 Field built the Marshall Field Wholesale Warehouse, the biggest and most famous of the city's department stores, taking up an entire city block; Pullman's company invented the Pullman sleeping car, revolutionizing railroad travel; and Palmer owned almost a mile of State Street, the city's main commercial district, and operated the luxurious Palmer House hotel, famous for the floor of its barbershop, which was tiled with silver dollars. Rudyard Kipling, who visited Chicago on more than one occasion, offered the following comment in *American Notes* from 1891, typical for foreigners not impressed with the city's vulgar display of money: "They told me to go to the Palmer House, which is overmuch gilded and mirrored, and there I found a huge hall of tessellated marble, crammed with people talking about money and spitting about everywhere. Other barbarians charged in and out of this inferno with letters and telegrams

true democratic spirit, and with it the tales of newspaper boys turned millionaires, of fortunes lost and won in the "pit" of the Board of Trade, and even if the newcomer should not make it all the way to the top, the city still had enough department stores and amusement halls to keep even the liveliest imagination busy.[36] To refined Easterners or Europeans, Chicago often seemed vulgar and rough, but for the population of the American Midwest, the city represented, in the words of literary historian Eric Homberger, "the pinnacle of sophistication and luxury" (152). It was the destination of choice for the thousands who, often spurred by the famous rags-to-riches novels of Horatio Alger, left the town, the farm and the coolly, going, as critic David R. Weimer has noted, "from known deprivations to hoped-for privileges" (66).[37] As a pure symbol of freedom, democracy and the possibility of success, Chicago was the American Dream incarnate, attracting people from all layers of society and most corners of the world. The popular image of the newly-arrived consisted of wide eyes, rosy cheeks and dim hopes of conquering the city, and, as nearly everyone in the city, successful or not, had gone through it in one way or

---

in their hands, and yet others shouted at each other. A man who had drunk quite as much as was good for him told me that this was 'the finest hotel in the finest city on God Almighty's earth.' By the way, when an American wishes to indicate the next county or state, he says, 'God A'mighty's earth.' This prevents discussion and flatters his vanity" (92).

36   James Gilbert has put the number of Chicago amusement halls during the 1880s at 250, and the number of saloons at approximately 5000, one for every 212 persons, and one per 127 in the slums (29).

37   Horatio Alger (1832–1899) was the author of more than one hundred novels with titles such as *Joe the Hotel Boy, Or Winning Out by Pluck* and *From Farm Boy to Senator: Being the History of the Boyhood and Manhood of Daniel Webster*. The total sales of his novels between the Civil War and the Great Depression have been estimated at an astounding ten million. For an interesting examination of the rags to riches philosophy as championed by Alger and others, and its impact on American culture and society in general, see Richard Weiss, *The American Myth of Success: From Horatio Alger to Norman Vincent Peale* (1969).

another, the experience possessed a certain degree of universality and soon found its way into countless works of contemporary literature.

During these formative years, Chicago was a city of business. Unlike other Midwestern urban centers, the city had not been founded as a response to the discovery of vast natural resources in the area, and was therefore not associated with steel, like Pittsburgh, with oil, like Cleveland, or with gold, like San Francisco. Rather, since Chicago came into being because of a fortunate array of geographical circumstances, combining to provide a location perfect for trade, the city was associated with business. "In Chicago," wrote Theodore Dreiser in *Sister Carrie*, "the two roads to distinction were politics and trade. In New York the roads were any one of a half-hundred" (232), making it clear that while other cities, and especially the nation's largest, might concern themselves with things other than power and commerce, and thus reflect in their literature a broad variety of themes, it was only natural that the literature of Chicago should be a literature of business and of the politics associated with it.

Literature is art, and in a society obsessed with the buying and selling, weighing and measuring of such tangible and commercial items as pork, corn, and wheat, the question of the position and status of art in the city soon arose. Chicago had, in the years preceding the World's Columbian Exposition, experienced an upward movement of the arts, born, as Kenny J. Williams has said, "out of a sincere and optimistic belief that in the days following the Fire of 1871 the city had a unique opportunity to mold itself into some type of ideal community" (1974, 74).[38] With the Fair coming and going, however, and with many of the initiatives of the past proving too slight for per-

---

38 Among the many short-lived attempts at founding organizations devoted to the arts were the Beethoven Club (1873–1885), the Mozart Club (1881–1886) and the Amateur Music Club, the latter limited to the women of society who could play the piano. For a fuller account of the upward movement, see Kenny J. Williams, *In the City of Men* (1974), chapter 2, and, of exceptional interest because of its contemporary perspective, Henry B. Fuller, "The Upward Movement in Chicago" (1897).

manence in the wake of the economic depression of 1894, the future for artistic expression in Chicago seemed uncertain.

In this way, part of the Chicago experience at the turn of the century became a combination of its roaring and unapologetic modernity, its look and smell of success, attracting new citizens by the millions, as well as its uncritical devotion to the accumulation of money through commerce, and, lastly, the insecurity and instability of its artistic activities. In literature, as in life, all of these themes collided and merged in the hustle and bustle of the modern metropolis. Here writers struggled from the very center of things to order and analyze their experience and, working determinedly toward their goals, succeeded in producing a vision uniquely their own, while distinctly Chicagoan.

Henry B. Fuller

Henry B. Fuller was a rarity among Chicago novelists and citizens in that he was a native to the city and therefore never experienced the magnetic attraction of the big city with the bright lights that affected so many of its early chroniclers. Born to a wealthy New England family in 1857, he could trace his ancestry to the Mayflower, and his grandfather had arrived in Chicago only sixteen years after its incorporation as a city.[39] A sensitive and rather lonely child who preferred to play with girls and create exciting worlds of melodrama with his "Swiss toy-village," Fuller grew up among the city's Old Settlers in an environment based on New England tradition and values.[40] Writing

---

39   Fuller was the last male descendant of Dr. Samuel Fuller of the Mayflower, and his grandfather, Henry Fuller, was a cousin of Margaret Fuller. The best critical biography of Fuller is Bernard R. Bowron, Jr., *Henry B. Fuller of Chicago: The Ordeal of a Genteel Realist in Ungenteel America* (1974), although it rather shortchanges Fuller's later, though admittedly weaker, career. For a more complete account of that period, with special (and fashionable) attention to Fuller's alleged homosexuality, refer to Kenneth Scambray, *A Varied Harvest: The Life and Works of Henry Blake Fuller* (1987).

40   In the unpublished article "Toy Village Theatricals" written, probably, in the late 1880s, Fuller gives what is perhaps the best account of his early child-

plays, essays and stories from an early age, Fuller dreamt about the romances of medieval Europe and made several trips abroad during his lifetime, both to steep himself in the atmosphere of the Old World and to get away from Chicago, a city he perceived as crude and bereft of culture. Being of a delicate disposition in an unrefined place, he later in life declared to his friend Hamlin Garland that if he could get away he "would go to Italy and never return" (Garland 1932, 25). He blamed his "damned New England conscience" for finally staying (Garland 1931, 369). His first novel, *The Chevalier of Pensieri-Vani*, was published in 1890, and is, along with his second, *The Châtelaine of La Trinité* from 1892, a tale of romantic escapism set in Europe, with characters bearing names such as Count Fin de Siècle and Baron Zeitgeist.[41] While these early novels won him critical acclaim in the East from the likes of Charles Eliot Norton and James Russell Lowell, Fuller, probably overcome with a sense of betraying his native city, decided to drive a stake, as he said, "at the extreme opposite end of the literary field."[42] In late 1893 he published a

hood, which is surrounded by some mystery as he rarely talked about it or discussed it in writing (MS, The Newberry Library, Chicago).

41   The first edition of *The Chevalier of Pensieri-Vani* was published under the pseudonym of Stanton Page, but Fuller's name appears on all subsequent editions.

42   Fuller had earlier, with the publication of such stories as "The Romance of a Middle-Aged Merchant and His Female Private Secretary" (1884) and "The Ballade of the Bank-Teller" (1881), shown his awareness that the mercantile nature of Chicago lent itself rather uneasily to romance. The quote is from a letter of July 4, 1893, to one Smith. In the letter, Fuller interestingly calls *The Châtelaine of La Trinité* "the best thing I have done, and the only thing I truly care for," although, he says, it "gave no new slant to the public feeling" (MS, The Newberry Library, Chicago). This latter remark might help explain his sudden shift from romance to realism, a style that was slowly coming into fashion through the encouragement of William Dean Howells. Also, in a letter written to Hamlin Garland at the time of the publication of *The Cliff-Dwellers*, Fuller wrote: "I have no fixed literary creed ... There are a good many ways to skin a cat, and the realistic way, I dare say, is as good a way as any" (quoted in Garland's *Roadside Meetings* (1930), 267). Fuller's apparent shift in literary styles has been

book of Chicago realism entitled *The Cliff-Dwellers*, having serialized it in *Harper's Weekly* during the summer of the World's Columbian Exposition, and with it introduced Chicago as material for serious fiction on the American literary map.

The Cliff-Dwellers begins with an "Introduction" in which Fuller establishes the setting and main theme of the novel, likening the urban landscape of Chicago to the Bad Lands of the American Southwest, with "great cañons" crossing each other with such "systematic rect-angularity" that "they are in general called simply—streets" (1). Fuller continues the conceit:

> Each of these cañons is closed in by a long frontage of towering cliffs, and these soaring walls of brick and limestone and granite rise higher and higher with each succeeding year, according as the work of erosion at their bases goes onward—the work of that seething flood of carts, carriages, omnibuses, cabs, cars, messengers, shoppers, clerks and capitalists, which surges with increasing violence for every passing day (1–2).

Centering his attention on one of these cliffs, appropriately called the Clifton, which stands "[f]rom the beer-hall in its basement to the barber-shop just under its roof" eighteen stories tall, Fuller moves inside, where elevators "ameliorate the daily cliff-climbing for the frail of physique and the pressed for time" (4). Calling the inhabitants a "tribe," he offers the following inventory:

> All told, it numbers about four thousand souls. It includes bankers, capitalists, lawyers, "promoters"; brokers in bonds, stocks, pork, oil, mortgages; real-estate people and railroad people and insur-

---

the subject of a large amount of the critical attention devoted to him, almost to the point of critics neglecting other aspects of his work. See for example Jeffrey Swanson, "'Flesh, Fish or Fowl': Henry Blake Fuller's Attitudes Toward Realism and Romanticism" (1974) and Kenneth Scambray, "The Romance in Decline: Realism in Henry Blake Fuller's *The Cliff-Dwellers*" (1978).

ance people—life, fire, marine, accident; a host of principals, agents, middlemen, clerks, cashiers, stenographers, and errand boys; and the necessary force of engineers, janitors, scrub-women, and elevator-hands (4–5).

Concluding that "the Clifton aims to be complete within itself" (5), Fuller sets the stage for perhaps the first thoroughly urban novel in American literature, using the unique features of the Chicago skyscraper as symbols for the small and hermetic communities constructed around the cliff-dwellers of the modern city. Many ways of life are concentrated within the building, and it consequently becomes a unique microcosm for Chicago itself, remarkably exemplifying the democratic spirit of the city, according to which all can enter the building on an equal footing, but where few eventually reach the top. Juxtaposing the extreme artificiality of the skyscraper with the cliffs and canyons of a natural environment, Fuller's central metaphor exposes the fundamental discrepancy between the city and all previous human experience, with the inhabitants nevertheless continuing their essentially tribal lives within, gathering as they do at the lunch-counter for the daily feast, and congregating at the cigar-stand in the lobby to "smoke the pipe of peace among themselves" (5).

The action of the novel is, as the introductory chapter suggests, largely set within the Clifton, and follows within it a representative group of characters as they go up and down the actual and symbolic elevators, overhearing conversations in the restaurants and barbershops along the way. The main character, George Ogden, is a young newcomer to the city from the East, working for Erastus Brainard, a wealthy but conscienceless banker whom Fuller introduces as "merely a financial appliance—one of the tools of the trade" (38), and who has never "lived for anything but business" (43).[43] Another charac-

---

43 Brainard in this respect sounds much like real-life Chicago tycoon Philip Armour, founder of the largest meat packing company in the nation, who admitted: "I have no other interest in life but my business. I do not want any more money; as you say, I have more than I want. I do not love the money. What

ter, Eugene McDowell, a real estate agent married to Ogden's sister, has taken an office on an upper floor next to that of the building's owner, Arthur J. Ingles, hoping in that way to be introduced to the great man. Finally, there is Cornelia McNabb, a socially ambitious girl working at the lunch-counter in the basement, an acquaintance of Ogden's, who reads the society pages and imagines herself in the place of Cecilia Ingles, the wife of the man in the top office.

There are several other characters in the novel, but it is this group that most clearly exemplifies Fuller's intentions, namely, to examine the effect of Chicago upon an assortment of people with various backgrounds, morals and dreams for the future. Shortly after arriving in the city, Ogden marries the frail Jessie Bradley of old settler background, but, as Fuller's biographer Bernard Bowron has explained, her "'corrupted' taste for social ostentation" (135) and determination to "entertain" soon leaves him penniless and forces him to steal from his employer, Brainard. The banker, on the other hand, once an honest downstate farmer, has been so overwhelmed by the commercial spirit of the Clifton that he writes "on business letterheads even to his family" (44) and breaks off relations with his son Marcus, whom he considers a failure due to his lack of financial success. McDowell, on the other hand, is "a poet—as every real-estate man should be" (104), and uses his skills to sell a low-lying swamp on the outskirts of town to Ann Wilde, the sister-in-law of Ogden's first Chicago contact. After the death of his father-in-law, McDowell begins to appropriate the various holdings of the estate, leaving Ogden with little to help his financial troubles. The lunch-counter-girl Cornelia, meanwhile, who times her breaks to coincide with those of the many powerful people working around her, marries Brainard's son Burton, and is soon on her way toward the top of the building.

A summary as detailed and complicated as this is necessary for the simple reason that the overly intricate plot is in fact partly the

---

I do love is the getting of it, the making it. All these years of my life I have put into this work, and now it is my life and I cannot give it up.... I do not read. I do not take any part in politics. What can I do?" (quoted in Dedmon, 186).

point. The close-knit structure of modern society, symbolized by the cramping together of people into dense anthills of human life, Fuller says, renders impossible any independent maneuvering without consequence. The Clifton, with its symbolic promise and hermetic nature, is in this way the central character of the novel, as the various characters see their lives conditioned by the almost naturalistic force of the building itself. In the end, as melodramatic developments such as murder, suicide, and the death of his spendthrift wife have saved him from financial ruin, Ogden visits the opera and sees for the first time Cecilia Ingles, and "his heart was constricted by the sight of her" (324). The last sentence of the novel reads: "It is for such a woman that one man builds a Clifton and that a hundred others are martyred in it" (324).

The novel was a moderate financial success but its impact on Chicago literature was immense. Critic Hjalmar Hjort Boyesen, in a *Cosmopolitan* review, noted that "Chicago has always seemed to me to be crying aloud for her chronicler, and she has, at last, found an able, though scarcely a sympathetic one, in Mr. Fuller" (374). William Dean Howells, always to be counted on for a review of the newest submission to the realistic canon, concluded in *Harper's Bazar* that "[a]s yet no New Yorker has begun to do as much for New York; no Bostonian for Boston" (1893, 883) as Fuller had done for Chicago with *The Cliff-Dwellers*. That contribution, however, was to become even more significant with the publication of Fuller's fourth novel in 1895, another foray into Chicago realism, entitled *With the Procession*.

By far the better novel, *With the Procession* is the story of old Chicago versus the new, a theme already touched upon with the marriage of George Ogden to Jessie Bradley in *The Cliff-Dwellers*. This time, however, Fuller does not lapse into melodrama near the end, and the novel is as remarkable an analysis of the conflict between social manners and personal ambition as American literature has produced outside of Henry James and Edith Wharton. Once again, as the title suggests, Fuller crafts a master metaphor large enough to encompass the whole of Chicago society for his literary purposes. The novel opens with a short passage chronologically belonging near the end of the narrative, describing the old Chicagoan patriarch David Marshall, a successful wholesale grocer, as he finally takes to his bed with failing health. The household, the narrator says, "viewed this action with more surprise than sympathy, and with more impatience than surprise" (3). He continues:

> It seemed like the breaking down of a machine whose trustworthiness had been hitherto infallible; his family were almost forced to the acknowledgement that he was but a mere human being after all [...] and their dismay was now such as might occur at the Mint if the great stamp were suddenly and of its own accord to cease its coinage of double-eagles and to sink into a silence of supine idleness (3).

Marshall, unpretentious and unimaginative, has lived all of his adult life in Chicago and has created his fortune by adhering to old-fashioned principles of treating his customers fairly. Occupying a house built before the Civil War and which survived the Great Fire of 1871, he is considered an outdated relic in the city, his standing long eclipsed by younger generations of ruthless capitalists for whom integrity and honor have little marketplace value. His life reduced to habits formed when "[t]he Chicago of his young married life had given him little reason for being abroad after half-past nine at night" (20), it has become impossible to convince him that the opportunities offered by the modern city are also available to him. Instead he has devoted his life to his business because, sounding for a moment like famous industrialist Philip Armour, it "was the only thing he could do [...] the sole thing which enabled him to look upon himself as a useful, stable, honored member of society" (21).[44] As a direct consequence of his public reticence, his family occupies a social position symbolized by their carriage, which, while showing "material and workmanship of the best order" (4), nevertheless proclaims to the world:

---

44 See preceding note.

I am not of the great world [...] I make no pretense to fashion. We are steady and solid, but we are not precisely in society, and we are far, very far indeed, from any attempt to cut a great figure. However, do not misunderstand our position; it is not that we are under, nor that we are exactly aside; perhaps we have been left just a little behind. Yes, that might express it—just a little behind (5).

The subject of the novel, in this way, becomes the Marshall family's sudden aspiration, through their daughter Jane, to keep up with the procession—that persistent march toward bigger and better things that is such an integral part of the city's culture—and reclaim their place in Chicago society. Jane's ambition is stirred when, upon visiting the rich and influential Susan Bates in order to secure funding for a pet charity project, she learns that her father was once a well-known figure in the city's higher circles and that she is also, therefore, in the words of Mrs. Bates, "one of *us*—the old settlers, the aborigines" (65). Taking Jane on a tour of her new and imposing mansion—built with money acquired fairly, it is made clear—Mrs. Bates shows off her numerous rooms and parlors, as well as the Grand Salon, as "the newspapers have decided to call it" (54), filled with "Louis Quinze" furniture, pianos, crystal chandeliers, and expensive European paintings, for, Mrs. Bates says, "after all, people of our position would naturally be expected to have a Corot" (57). Buying her books in sets, so that the walls are lined with "twenty or thirty yards of Scott [...] and enough Encyclopædia Britannica to reach around the corner and back again" (49), it is clear that Mrs. Bates, in typical Chicago fashion, is not as interested in the artistic merit of cultural artifacts as in the social prestige associated with them.

Taking an interest in the Marshalls, Mrs. Bates visits the old man in his office, advising him on how to fight his way back into prominence. "Make it something that people can *see*" (95), she says, convincing him to build a magnificent new house in a fashionable neighborhood, to construct a tall new office building for his business, and to underwrite a student dormitory to be named after him at the new university campus. "Keep up with the procession is my motto," she tells Jane, "and head it if you can. I *do* head it, and I feel that I'm where I belong" (58). The Marshalls, however, are not where they belong, and the family's eventual failure to keep up with the procession of modern Chicago is evidenced by their new house proving less desirable than their old, the existing office building being unglamorously expanded, and by the plans for the university hall being scrapped upon the death of Marshall. These failures illustrate Fuller's belief that they would have done better, as critic Robert C. Bray has concluded, to "learn the lessons of their old-Chicago past in order to reject any practice of pecuniary emulation of the upstart rich around them" (101).

According to the novel's slightly reductive view, Chicago before the Great Fire was a city inhabited by industrious and honest businessmen for whom morality and ethics were important words, in business as well as personal matters. The flocking of other kinds of people to the city after the conflagration, attracted by the promise of easy money in the new city being built, and the futility of the older generation's attempt to keep up with their procession, is Fuller's main theme. As for the depiction of the ambiguous position of culture in the city, Fuller uses the example of Mrs. Bates's Corot and her "[s]ets—sets—sets" (49) of books to make it clear that, in Chicago, art is not "an integral part of the great frame of things" (118), and that it can only exist, as critic G. Thomas Couser has pointed out, as "an adornment or symbol of economic success" (33).[45]

Throughout his entire career, Fuller was deeply involved with the prospects of art and culture in a city that had, to use writer Waldo

---

45 Truesdale, the son of David Marshall, having just returned from a grand tour of the Continent, is dismayed with the cultural life as he finds it in Chicago, and one suspects him of humorously echoing Fuller's own sentiments regarding his native city: "'No journals,' pursued Truesdale; 'no demi-tasse, no clientèle, no leisure. No,' he added, with the idea of a more general summing up, 'nor any excursions; nor any general market; nor any military; nor even any morgue. And five francs for a cab. *Quelle Ville!*'" (117).

Frank's phrase about America at large, "sprung so nakedly [...] from a direct and conscious material impulse" (120). In an uncharacteristically optimistic 1897 essay in the *Atlantic Monthly*, entitled "The Upward Movement in Chicago," he catalogued the various undertakings to bring culture to the city and ended by concluding that "a high intellectual status seems assured" (547). Just two years later, in an article in the *Bookman* called "Art in America," he argued that the very nature of the country itself was against artistic expression and called for "a halt on misapplied energy. We are under no obligation to create artificial needs and difficulties for ourselves [...] let art wait outside" (223–224).[46] This apparent change in perspective is emblematic for Fuller's disillusionment with the city, and in a collection of three short stories, published as *Under the Skylights* in 1901, Fuller brought his despair to an ironic and provocative apex. The stories are slightly masked send-ups of the Chicago artistic circle, of which he was occasionally a part, and especially the first story, "The Downfall of Abner Joyce," is a blatantly obvious satire of Hamlin Garland.[47] The story lampoons the titular character, a "masterful, self-centred creature" (116) who calls himself a "veritist" and is campaigning for Western art, insisting that the local painters devote their time to portraits of milkmaids instead of the customary marquises. Ironically, as happened to Garland, his ideals are soon softened by city living and, fulfilling a character's prophecy that "[h]e will become quite like the

46   Of the native difficulties listed by Fuller, the most interesting is perhaps the nation's Anglo-Saxon heritage, leaving the population, as he says, "without any devotion to general ideas" (218). He continues, later in the same essay: "Whatever success the English have had in art has come, as Mr. Henry James somewhere states, from their fondness for overcoming difficulties, and the chief of these difficulties is a fundamental inaptitude for art" (219).

47   Garland himself, a lifelong friend of Fuller, oddly did not seem to mind, but noted years later in *Roadside Meetings* (1930) that Fuller had "depicted our artist colony with quiet humor and authority," and that "[h]e liked us, but he measured and weighed us" (268).

rest of us in time" (130), he eventually settles into a comfortable life of fame and luxury.

The second story, "Little O'Grady vs. The Grindstone," chronicles the attempts made by a group of artists to get the commission for the decoration of a new Chicago bank, each of them compromising their initially lofty ideals as fast as possible, until the manager of the bank finally exclaims: "To hell with art! [...] What I wanted to do was to advertise my business" (289). In Chicago, art is merely an embellishment on financial accomplishment, and while criticizing the artists for their willingness to be corrupted, Fuller is also reproachful of the city, which is in a sense the ultimate cause of the barren artistic environment and has left them with virtually no other outlets for their art.

The final story is the weakest of the three and concerns a farmhand who obtains a book of cultural theory reminiscent of Garland's *Crumbling Idols*, inspiring him to paint realistic pictures of squashes and frame them with fencing board. As is to be expected, his works become highly successful in Chicago society where they are praised for their realism, as well as for being "simple, tangible, familiar, appealing" (350)—more or less cataloguing the requirements articulated by Garland for local art. A major department store pays $500 for an immense painting of a squash to be displayed in its show window, while claiming to the public to have paid ten thousand dollars for it. Here Fuller despairingly concluded, according to critic Elwood P. Lawrence, that "the materialism rampant in Chicago in the 1890s stifled any desire on the part of its inhabitants for what are sometimes called 'the finer things in life'" (143). Chicago art, in this way, becomes a simple commodity, and its artistic quality is eclipsed by its monetary value, illustrating yet again the commercial spirit permeating the entire city.

Despite their satiric intent, these stories are comparatively minor achievements, and Fuller seems overcome throughout with a sense of hopelessness in the face of the gigantic commercial machine. It is as if he has given up on his attempt, as he wrote to William Dean Howells in 1895, to "raise this dirt pile to some dignity and credit" (quoted in Martin, 249) and he was to publish only sporadically after the lukewarm reception of *Under the Skylights*.[48] Critic Robert Morss Lovett has suggested about Fuller that "there was war in his members; he wanted to live and write as an European, and he knew that he must live and write as an American. Undoubtedly his material went sour on him" (17). Fuller himself, in another letter to Howells, called Chicago a "repellant town" and admitted to having "no great liking for the environment I must depict, and no great zest for life as it is lived. In such circumstances should a man write at all?" (quoted in Bowron, 217).[49]

The case of Henry B. Fuller is a curious one in American literature. A brightly shining star in the literary sky of the 1890s, Fuller seems to have been so completely at odds with his environment—

---

48   In the letter, Fuller also confessed: "Really I write about this town neither because I like it or hate it, but because I can't escape it and because I am so ashamed of it. If you are condemned to residence on a muckheap wouldn't you too edit it? Wouldn't you want to give it some credit, some standing (*as a muckheap*) by ordering, formulating, characterizing its various delectabilities?" (quoted in Daniel Aaron's introduction to Robert Herrick's *The Memoirs of an American Citizen* (1963), xi).

49   The answer to this question, apparently, was yes, for after two decades of near-silence, during which he published mostly book reviews and the occasional critical essay, there again began to appear novels and books of travel bearing Fuller's name. Of these, the two Chicago novels *On the Stairs*, from 1918, and *Bertram Cope's Year*, published one year later, are of the greatest interest. The first chronicles the simultaneous rise and fall of two Chicago businessmen in naturalistic terms reminiscent of the novels of Theodore Dreiser, and the second concerns itself with the relationship between a young graduate student and an older man, and is set in an environment modeled on the University of Chicago campus. Both novels, however, suffer from their author's apparent lack of interest and have an air of being half-finished, half-realized works. Ironically, *Bertram Cope's Year*, because of its early treatment of what might be conceived as homosexuality, is the most recent of Fuller's novels to be reissued. The afterword by Andrew Solomon in the 1998 Turtle Point Press edition enthusiastically makes the most of this, calling the novel "a sterling study in the kind of ambivalence that must have characterized Fuller's own life" (298).

while at the same time unable to leave it behind for longer than the occasional few months of European travel—that he finally, and inevitably, burned out. His Chicago novels, obscure and out of print as they remain today, are nevertheless important because they were fundamental in putting the city on the American literary map, and proved that refined and thoughtful literature could be written about a city that was anything but.[50]

Robert Herrick

If it can be said of Henry B. Fuller that he disliked Chicago, and that he seems never to have made his peace with the city, it must be said of Robert Herrick, another early Chicago novelist, that he despised his adopted city with a hate so fervent that, as Kenneth S. Lynn has remarked, it "burns and scorches every page" (208). Unlike Fuller, Herrick was an outsider to the city. Born in Cambridge, Massachusetts in 1868 and educated at Harvard—where he edited the literary magazine with Robert Morss Lovett and William Vaughn Moody—Herrick was recruited by the English Department at the newly founded University of Chicago in 1893, where he was to hold a teaching position for the next thirty years, all the while publishing more than two dozen novels.[51] A New Englander by birth and intellectual disposition, Herrick felt disgusted with the overt commercialism of Chicago where, he wrote in his unpublished autobiography, "[e]verybody knew more or less what everybody was after, and there was little of the beauty and old social customs that soften the harsher aspects of a people whose energies are centered upon 'SUCCESS'" (77–

---

50   Fuller's importance as an early realist and precursor to the novels of Frank Norris and Theodore Dreiser is testified to in a 1932 article by Dreiser in the *American Spectator* entitled "The Great American Novel." Dreiser misdates *With the Procession* as having appeared in 1886, but determines that "[i]f there is such a thing as the father of American realism, Henry B. Fuller is that man" (1).

51   The best—and only—critical biography of Herrick is Blake Nevius's *Robert Herrick: The Development of a Novelist* (1962).

78).[52] This lack of mystique and social customs in the city of "fat-fed capitalists" (1970, 17) and their never-ending "chase for the nimble dollar" (1913, 168) supplied Herrick with material for several novels and, read together, they display an impressive unity of theme, chronicling the systematic destruction of human idealism by the "titanic, heartless embrace" of the city (1913, 129).

In *The Web of Life*, published in 1900 and set during the economic depression in the years following the World's Columbian Exposition, Herrick chronicles the moral awakening of a young and idealistic Chicago surgeon as he refuses to establish a fashionable practice and gradually becomes disgusted with what he calls the city's "aristocracy of THOSE WHO HAVE" (139). Extricating himself from society by consciously casting off class, profession and social relations, Dr. Howard Sommers trades in his membership at the country club for a life of poverty following the death of one of his patients, whose penniless wife, Alves, he has earlier become romantically involved with. Escaping for a while to small-town Wisconsin, the pair nevertheless realizes the need for Sommers to return to Chicago and look for work, something that proves nearly impossible because, by having publicly rejected his former friends and relations in his desire to "start with life on the simplest, crudest base" (194), he has in effect become a *persona non grata* in the city. Living first in a boarding house and later in an abandoned ticket-booth left over from the Fair—and characteristically built in the style of a Greco-Roman temple—the couple struggle to make ends meet. Eventually Sommers sinks into inertia and discovers the true meaning of being powerlessly apart from society, a condition he nevertheless ultimately accepts, reminding himself that he has "chosen to be of the multitude whom the machine ground"

---

52   MS, entitled "Myself," The University of Chicago Library. It is interesting to note the degree to which Herrick's sentiments (and capitalization) resemble those of William James, who stated, in a letter to H. G. Wells, that "the moral flabbiness born of the exclusive worship of the bitch-goddess SUCCESS. That—with the squalid cash interpretation put on the word success—is our national disease" (260).

(201). Alves, meanwhile, thinking herself a burden to Sommers and an obstacle to his happiness, sacrificially drowns herself. This marks "the end of his little personal battle with the world, the end of judging and striving, the end of revolt" (315), and rekindles his desire to enter back into the "fretwork, unsolvable world of little and great, of domineering and incompetent wills" (316). Readjusting himself to society, Sommers discovers that while he was right about its essential shortcomings, extricating himself from it was not the solution to his problems, as the decision left him with nothing but complete and utter powerlessness. As Robert C. Bray has pointed out, he had "[i]n his headlong initial reaction against the evils of unenlightened wealth [...] rushed past, without noticing it, that crucial middle ground of American life" (115), and he must finally and consequently reconcile himself with being common, and with having, as Herrick calls it, a small, "old-fashioned kind of practice" (349).

Sharing Fuller's preference for the older generation of businessmen, Herrick's book warns that Chicago has forgotten how to be average and has instead, by its uncritical devotion to money and success, become a city of extremes, of "the brutal rich" and "the brutalized poor" (167). As a character bluntly says near the end: "Every boy and girl in this country is told from the first lesson in the cradle, over and over, that success is the one great and good thing in life. The people here [in Chicago] are young and strong, and you can't blame them if they interpret that text a little crudely" (336). It is a national disease, then, but the raw nature and lack of tradition in Chicago intensifies those very evils that in other—and especially Eastern—cities are kept moderately at bay by a framework of social customs and individual morality, and it is only by actively searching out the average, and finding peace in mediocrity and lowered ambitions, that the city can ever hope to rise above its inherent tawdriness.

With *The Web of Life*, Herrick found a main theme in his distaste for the city in which he lived. Another variation constitutes the main premise of his 1904 novel, *The Common Lot*, which tells the story of young architect Jackson Hart, educated in Paris and the East, who, his schooling having come to an end, reluctantly returns to his native Chicago from what he calls "the beauty, the wonder, the joy of Europe" (19). When a wealthy uncle passes away, Hart becomes convinced that he stands to inherit enough money to enable him to "flee to those other more sympathetic parts of the earth which he knew so well how to enjoy!" (6), and he begins to plan for a life of leisure. The uncle, however, seemingly in a last attempt to undo his lifelong exploitation of labor, bequeaths his large fortune to the establishment of an industrial school for the "children of workingmen" (32) and Hart is forced to cast his lot with the ranks of "toiling, sweating humanity" (30) in the "hard game" of life (38). This game, he realizes, is no less hard for the artist or the professional man than for anyone else, as is explained in a speech made by an older member of his club:

> Time has been when it meant something of honor for a man to be a member of one of the learned professions. Men were content to take part of their pay in honor and respect from the community. There's no denying that's all changed now. We measure everything by one yardstick, and that is money. So the able lawyer and the able doctor have joined the race with the mob for the dollars (55).

The corruption of the professional in a competitive capitalistic society thus seems a given, and Hart soon realizes that in this world "there isn't much room for sentiment and fine ideas and philanthropy until you are old, and have earned your pile, and done your neighbor out of his in the process" (87). Embodying the role of artist as well as professional, Hart's situation is further complicated. Originally aspiring to high ideals of aesthetic expression acquired at the École des Beaux-Arts in Paris, he finds that in Chicago art is "only good when it succeeds. It doesn't live unless it can succeed in pleasing people, in making money. I see that now! Chicago has taught me that much in two years" (87). Having begun in a relatively low position in an established firm, he now determines to start his own company and tells his wife: "If I get some big commissions, and put up a lot of skyscrapers or mills, why, I shall have won out. What does any one care for the kind of work you do? It's the price it brings every time!" (88). Hart thereby resigns himself to the systematic corrosion of artistic and professional principles that Herrick has set in motion, and of which Chicago is the catalyst.

Herrick is a moralist, and consequently the program requires that Hart, following his newly acquired sentiments to their logical end, must err, repent, and finally learn from his mistakes, much as Dr. Sommers realized his failure in *The Web of Life*. Commissioned to head the construction of the school endowed by his uncle, Hart churns out an imposing but imitative design, "straight from the Hôtel de Ville" (260), signaling the fading of his "sense of the fine, the noble, the restrained" amid the "clamor and excitement and gross delight of living" in Chicago (262). The city not only numbs artistic powers, but it also offers ample opportunities for unlawful behavior. Soon Hart is involved with a disreputable contractor who convinces him to cut corners in their common projects, including a hotel so badly constructed that it bursts into flames shortly after having been finished, causing the death of several guests and launching an investigation to bring the responsible to justice. In melodramatic fashion, once again, Hart witnesses the fire and is so stricken with grief and remorse that he immediately, and before the authorities can find him, leaves Chicago and wanders, as if in a daze, out into the country. There he experiences a spiritual rebirth, and for the first time he understands the true nature of things: "In the world where he had lived this passion had a dignified name; it was called enterprise and ambition. But now he saw it for what it was,—greed and lust and nothing more. It was in the air of the city which he had breathed for eight years. [...] In his pride he had justified knavery by Success" (338). With help from his upstanding wife, he realizes that he must face the consequences of his wrongdoings, but Herrick's project has no use for a man in prison, and the political influence of Hart's cousin thus saves him from the Grand Jury.

Had he been indicted and found guilty, Hart would have lost the opportunity to learn the lesson Herrick provides at the end of the novel, one foreshadowed by the title and reminiscent of the closing pages of *The Web of Life*. Arguing that the relentless struggle to get ahead in life is to be blamed for their troubles, Hart's wife takes it upon herself to spell things out: "We think it a disgrace to stay in the ranks, to work for the work's sake, to bear the common lot, which is to live humbly and labor! Don't let us struggle that way any longer, dear. It is wrong,—It is a curse. It will never give us happiness—never!" (402). As if to make sure the moral cannot be missed, she repeats a few pages later: "how Chicago had moulded him and had left his nature set in a hard crust of prejudice. The great industrial city where he had learned the lesson of life throttled the finer aspirations of men like a remorseless giant, converting its youth into iron-clawed beasts of prey, answering to the one hoarse cry, 'Success, Success, Success!'" (406). Taking a job with his former employer, Hart goes back to work. It is important, however, that he does not begin at the bottom, as that would imply that he is merely starting out for the top all over again. Instead he opts for "a career of real spiritual significance, if of little outward display" (419), which allows him to sink into "the insignificance of the common lot, so much praised by the poets, so much despised by our good Americans of the 'strenuous' school" (420). Both in *The Common Lot* and *The Web of Life*, Herrick supplies a conclusion suggesting that a change in individual morality is necessary for the spiritual regeneration of the fallen society that Chicago represented to him. As literary historian Bernard Duffey has written about the novel, although the evil lies "in the human seed," it is "brought to flower by the hothouse of Chicago life" (119), and if a civilized society is to be attained, Herrick argues, men must stop their blind striving for the ever illusive success and content themselves with being average.

Having exhausted this mode of literary firebrand preaching, Herrick tried another approach for his next Chicago novel. Although his theme remained largely unchanged, *The Memoirs of an American Citizen*, published a year later, used the tropes belonging to the biography of the businessman to tell his by now familiar story of the corrupting power of success.[53] Narrated in a plain and unadorned style,

---

53 For a full discussion of the ways in which Herrick inverts and satirizes

the first-person novel is the fictive autobiography of Chicago meat-packer Van Harrington, recounting his rise from homeless youth to influential millionaire and eventual senator in true Horatio Alger fashion. This field proved a fertile one for Herrick, and the main achievement of the novel is the way in which he resists the temptation to editorialize as directly as he had done in his earlier Chicago fiction. Instead, he trusts his readers to draw their own conclusions as they witness the systematic self-exposure of Harrington with his empty morals and uncritical acceptance of the pseudo-scientific principles of social Darwinism.

True to his kind, Harrington understands early in life how the system works, as all eventual Chicago millionaires must:

> While I was sweating on that farm I saw the folly of running against common notions about property. I came to the conclusion that if I wanted what my neighbor considered to be his, I must get the law to do the business for me. For the first time it dawned on me how wonderful is that system which shuts up one man in jail for taking a few dollars' worth of truck that doesn't belong to him, and honors the man who steals his millions—if he robs in the legal way! (22).

Making this his creed, Harrington is soon on his way to 1870s Chicago, and the city proves a virtual El Dorado of opportunity as he bribes, cheats, and blackmails his way to the top of a major meatpacking company. Reading Darwin and Spencer "and a lot more hard nuts" along the way (52), he justifies his dealings with a characteristic shrug of the shoulders and a firm belief that "the world is for the strong [...] and I am one of them (77). This, Herrick is sure to make clear, is especially true of Chicago where, as a character informs Harrington, "[n]o one asks, if you *succeed*" (141). The novel reads more or less like

the biography of the heroic businessman, using examples from works on An-drew Carnegie, Jay Gould and Philip Armour, see Wm. M. Phillips, "Tropes and Parodies of Capitalist Biography: Carnegie's 'Gospel of Wealth' vs. Herrick's *Memoirs*" (1999).

the literature it parodies, consisting mostly of lengthy descriptions of deals, takeovers, and all the other maneuvers of modern finance capitalism, with the hero-author taking immense pride in his various exploitations of the marketplace, seemingly unaware of the immoral nature of his actions. But, as he argues in a striking passage, concepts such as integrity and morality are of another, and older, world:

> That beautiful scheme of things which the fathers of our country drew up in the stage-coach days had proved itself inadequate in a short century […] [and] we men who did the work of the world, who developed the country, who were the life and force of the times, could not be held back by the swaddling-clothes of any political or moral theory. Results we must have: good results; and we worked with the tools we found at hand (191).

Demanding those results, of course, is Chicago, and, to be sure, Harrington is only working toward the same goal as everyone else: financial and material success. Herrick's main criticism, therefore, is once again directed at a society that, as critic Wm. M. Phillips has argued, "saw rewards going to those who used the new economic system for individualistic profit rather than those who played by the older 'rules'" (19). The ambiguity implicit in the meatpacker's statements is at the heart of the book, and it becomes clear that the argument quoted above speaks simultaneously for Herrick as well as Harrington. The difference between the two men is that the former despairs at a society that has become morally bankrupt, while the latter accepts it as a given and uses it uncritically to his own advantage, deluding himself that he is essentially a heroic figure: "There were my plants, my car line, my railroads, my elevators, my lands – all good tools in the infinite work the world [sic]. Conceived for good or for ill, brought into being by fraught or daring – what man could judge *their* worth? There they were, a part of God's great world. They were done; and mine was the hand" (266).

    The Memoirs of an American Citizen, with its ironic narrative voice and unbridled critique of the hollowness of the American Dream of success, was Herrick's last novel set explicitly in Chicago, although many of his themes were to appear unchanged in later works. His 1910 novel *A Life for a Life*, for example, is a strictly allegorical version of a similar story, following a youth as he enters The City, attracted "as the candle draws the moth" (44) by a brightly lighted sign saying, simply, "SUCCESS" (44). He quickly rises in society but the novel ends with an apocalyptic yet purifying fire that destroys both the city and all the major characters, leaving only a timid hope that a new and better city might someday arise from the ashes.

Though even the best of Robert Herrick's novels suffer from having been constructed more as statements of intense distaste than out of a feeling of artistic necessity, his refusal to romanticize economic ambition and his continuous attempt to write what Kenneth S. Lynn has memorably called "the great American antisuccess novel" (228) deserves more credit than it has received. He tirelessly endeavored to expose the empty promise of Success made by Chicago at the turn of the century, and in doing so vividly captured a historical moment characterized by shifting values. As Robert C. Bray has noted, Herrick's Chicago "was made by the wrong sort of men for the wrong reasons, and the wrong sort of men continued to be made by the humanly unhealthy influence of the city" (110). His Chicago novels bear witness to the passion of a man so out of tune with his environment that he could do nothing but record his failure to relate to it. While Henry B. Fuller managed to keep Chicago at intellectual bay and disappeared to Europe for a few months from time to time, Herrick's literary rage burned so intensely that it intensified with each new novel until it finally took the form of allegory and eventually died out. After finishing his preoccupation with the city, he never wrote of it again and ended his life as Government Secretary of the Virgin Islands, confessing to a friend that he had misspent his life as an artist and thinker, and that his true vocation had all along been that of a man of action.[54]

---

54   This letter is mentioned but not referenced in Bernard Duffey, *The Chicago Renaissance in American Letters: A Critical History* (1954), 122.

Another writer fascinated by the man of action was Frank Norris, who was born in Chicago in 1870 but moved with his family to Oakland and later San Francisco in 1884. The son of a wealthy jewelry merchant so preoccupied with his business that he rarely had time to see his family, the young Norris studied to become a painter in Paris and later entered Berkeley and Harvard, spending his time writing poems, plays and novels instead of attending classes. Setting most of his books in and around San Francisco—such as *McTeague*—he decided in 1899 to try his hand at writing a trilogy of novels forming the story of a crop of wheat from its production in California, through its sale and distribution at the Chicago Board of Trade, and finally its consumption as bread in Europe. Characteristically deciding that the series should be "straight naturalism with all the guts I can get into it," he named it "The Trilogy of The Epic of the Wheat" and set to work on the first volume, which appeared as *The Octopus* in 1901. In it Norris heavily criticized the *laissez-faire* capitalism which was a result of a blind faith in social Darwinism as a valid and dominating economic principle.[55] The final volume, to be called *The Wolf*, was never completed as Norris died suddenly in October 1902, but the second novel in the series appeared posthumously in January 1903 as *The Pit*, and was subtitled "A Story of Chicago."[56]

For Norris, Chicago equaled business. This point is made clear at the very beginning of the novel as its heroine, Massachusetts native

55   The quote from Norris appears in Kevin Starr's introduction to the 1994 Penguin Books edition of *The Octopus*, xviii.

56   The novel originally carried the subtitle "A Romance of Chicago" when it was serialized in the *Saturday Evening Post* in the months preceding its publication in book form. Norris perceived naturalism as being midway between realism and romanticism, which might help explain the apparent discrepancy; but perhaps his publishers feared that the subtitle would draw attention away from the business aspects of the novel. For a detailed discussion of this and several other textual differences between the two versions, many of which were not approved by Norris before his death, see Gwendolyn Jones, "Frank Norris's *The Pit*: 'A Romance of Chicago' and 'A Story of Chicago'" (1996).

Laura Dearborn, attends an opera at the Auditorium where the conversation among the men soon turns to the dealings of the day at the Board of Trade. As it penetrates even into the finest culture the city has to offer, there is no escaping the business aspect of Chicago. On her way home from the concert, Laura learns this lesson as her carriage passes through the commercial district, which is bustling with activity even though it is well past midnight. Chicago is truly the city that never sleeps, and Laura, looking down LaSalle Street, sees the "black, grave, monolithic" Board of Trade Building itself, crouching as it does "like a monstrous sphinx with blind eyes" (39). Powerfully ominous as this image is, *The Pit* takes its name from the trading room inside, which contains "some great, some resistless force [...] a great whirlpool, a pit of roaring waters" that makes its powers felt "[a]ll through the Northwest, all through the central world of the Wheat" (72). Here, the wheat of the nation is bought and sold at prices determined by the speculation of a few ruthless traders such as Curtis Jadwin, the man Laura will eventually meet and marry. Soon after their marriage, Jadwin becomes increasingly preoccupied with his work at the Board of Trade and eventually plans to corner the market.

The stage thus set for what Carl S. Smith has called "the businessman as the author, producer, director and leading actor in the urban drama" (62), the novel follows Jadwin's attempt to control the market and thereby the mighty force of the wheat itself. This feat proves almost impossible as he is "hypnotised and soothed by the sound of the distant rumble of the Pit" (75) and is sucked further and further into "the fury of the Maëlstrom, into the chaotic spasm of a world-force, a primeval energy, blood-brother of the earthquake and the glacier, raging and wrathful that its power should be braved by some pinch of human spawn that dared raise barriers across its courses" (73).[57] Nearing the end, as his marriage is quickly disintegrating,

57 It is interesting to compare Norris's description of the hypnotic influence and raw power of the Board of Trade with one found in Hamlin Garland's uncharacteristically impressionistic "Chicago Studies," which were written in

Jadwin must learn, as cultural historian Richard Lehan has pointed out, that "even abstract matters like wheat speculation are governed by laws that ultimately come back to nature" (197), and he is therefore obliged to admit that he is a mere instrument of the forces at work: "You think I am willfully doing this! You don't know, you haven't a guess. I corner the wheat! Great heavens, it is the wheat that has cornered me! The corner made itself. I happened to stand between two sets of circumstances, and they made me do what I've done" (249).[58]

Even though the small and insignificant personal world of Jadwin is in the end destroyed by the wheat and his corner is broken, he remains a curiously heroic figure. A former opponent remarks near the end: "It was the wheat himself that beat him; no combination of men could have done it […] he was a bigger man than the best of

the mid-1890s but remained unpublished until being included in a 1964 article by James B. Stronks. Garland writes, in a passage entitled "The Wheat Exchange": "Standing in the very heart of Chicago the listening ear grows aware of a deep, unintermitting, all-pervasive, ominous roar … This roar is the voice of the middle west, for this is the sound of the wheat-pit in daily clamor. It is electric, vast and sorrowful, this sound which reaches you as you pass in the street—this shrill clamor, this strange, intermittent, spasmodic, many-threaded, loosely-flung banner of tumult," 51. The similarities between the two descriptions suggest the distinctive experience associated with the Board of Trade as a Chicago symbol. For a full discussion of Garland's manuscripts, as well as the sketches themselves, see Stronks, "A Realist Experiments with Impressionism: Hamlin Garland's 'Chicago Studies'" (1964).

58   Van Wyck Brooks, among others, has pointed out the similarity between this speech and one made by the railroad-magnate Shelgrim in *The Octopus*, and indeed Norris never seems afraid of repeating himself for emphasis, with *The Pit* containing several other passages that are merely rewrites of the same theme. Shelgrim, when accused of exploiting the farmers, defiantly states, with Norris's trademark fondness for upper-case emphasis: "What do I count for? Do I build the Railroad? You are dealing with forces, young man, when you speak of Wheat and the Railroads, not with men. There is the Wheat, the supply. It must be carried to feed the People. There is the demand. The Wheat is one force, the Railroad another, and there is the law that governs them—supply and demand. Men have only little to do in the whole business" (576).

us" (347), and though Jadwin is destined to lose in the same way as most protagonists of American naturalism, he nevertheless achieves a certain grandeur simply by daring to challenge the raw and overwhelming powers of nature. It is nevertheless surprising how Norris, throughout the novel—especially in the light of his accomplishments in *The Octopus*—seems uncritical of the essentially immoral financial framework he exposes along the way, and of what Floyd Dell has called Jadwin's "insane way of doing business" within it (1913, 271). The speculator is Norris's modern American hero, fighting superhuman battles of epic proportions against invincible adversaries, but the novel suffers from his automatic admiration for all things larger than man himself. Consequently, while Jadwin is meant to be very different from the greedy and morally corrupt businessmen of Fuller and Herrick, he appears in the end as only a slightly more distinguished version of the by now familiar type. Implicit in the novel is the idea that Chicago was perhaps the only city in America offering, as Robert C. Bray has noted, "sufficient latitude for a heroic businessman to flex his muscles" (144). Moreover, the sheer magnitude of the undertaking is typical of the new scale on which things were done in Chicago in the years around the turn of the century, and *The Pit* therefore makes its plot an almost natural function of its setting. One man controlling the world's supply of wheat? Only in Chicago.[59]

Theodore Dreiser

For Theodore Dreiser, Chicago sang the song of unlimited promise, and he sang with it. Born in Terre Haute, Indiana, in 1871 to a stern

---

59 According to Hugh Dalziel Duncan, Norris actually based his story of the attempted corner on real events: "Jadwin, the hero of 'the Battle of the Street,' had his counterpart in Benjamin P. Hutchinson ('Old Hutch'), the Chicago grain plunger who controlled the world's wheat during his great September *coup* in 1888. Local newspaper reports of 1888 are scarcely less dramatic than the novel of 1902 [sic]. In such stories we read that whenever 'Old Hutch' even engaged in conversation in the pit, all conversation died and business stopped" (1965, 91).

and pious German Catholic father and a sympathetic mother with seemingly endless energy to help and encourage her ten children, Dreiser grew up in poverty. In *Dawn*, one of several autobiographies, he remembered collecting coal along the railroad tracks to help keep the family warm during his earliest years. His imagination fed by two sisters and a brother already in Chicago, Dreiser went to the city at the age of fifteen and supported himself as a dishwasher and shipping clerk before securing work as a regular feature writer for the less than distinguished Chicago *Globe*.[60] Reading Eugene Field's highly successful "Sharps and Flats" column in the *Daily News* influenced his early work as a journalist, which consisted mainly of chronicling the lives of the city's richest and most influential citizens, Philip Armour and Marshall Field among them. Writing intermittently at the same time for a magazine simply and bluntly called *Success*, Dreiser found new things around every corner to stir his appetite for city life. As he recalled in *Newspaper Days* (1922), "It is given to some cities, as to some lands, to suggest romance, and to me Chicago did that hourly. It sang, I thought, and in spite of what I deemed my various troubles—small enough as I now see them—I was singing with it" (1).[61] Witnessing on a daily basis the miraculously good fortune of others, he was himself denied the prizes of capitalism of which he dreamt and soon became aware of the evident duality present in the city, between the otherworldly displays of success and "the peculiarly human or realistic atmosphere" (1). "I think I grasped Chicago in its larger material if not in its more complicated mental aspects" (20), Dreiser explained, and it is precisely this all-encompassing vision of the "vital and determined" city (296), as he wrote in *Dawn*, coupled with his

---

60   Dreiser's brother Paul, changing his last name to Dresser in a bid to sound more American, was the composer of several of the era's most popular songs, such as "My Gal Sal" and the sentimental ballad "On the Banks of the Wabash," the latter of which was turned into a movie in 1923 and is now the Indiana state song.

61   The image of Chicago as singing to its inhabitants was one of Dreiser's favorites. For other examples see *Dawn*, 156, and *The Titan*, 4, 6.

recognition of the raw forces at work in society, that gives such power and unity of theme to his first novel, published in 1900 and called, somewhat puzzlingly, *Sister Carrie.*[62]

The opening chapter of the novel is entitled, appropriately and ominously, "The Magnet Attracting: A Waif Among Forces," and is a small masterpiece of Chicago writing, chronicling perhaps the single most emblematic experience offered by the city in the last decades of the nineteenth century, and introducing all of Dreiser's major themes.[63] The first few sentences set the stage for the rest of the novel:

---

62   According to Dreiser, the title came into his head one day and, having no idea what it meant, he wrote the book to find out. Carrie's family, however, after her initial stay with her sister in Chicago, is curiously never mentioned again, and she herself is only referred to as "Sister Carrie" on six occasions, the last time being on page 62 of a 400-page novel, suggesting that as the novel progressed, Dreiser grew less interested in this aspect of his protagonist's life. The ambiguous nature of the word, however, at the same time implies that Carrie's moral undoing does not exclude her from being referred to as a "Sister."

63   Two different editions of *Sister Carrie* exist. After the novel was rejected by Harper Brothers on the grounds of not being "sufficiently delicate to depict without offense to the reader the continued illicit relations of the heroine" (quoted in E. L. Doctorow's introduction to the 1992 Bantam Books edition, vii), Dreiser's wife Sara and his close friend Arthur Henry assisted him in editing out the offensive material, and it was not until the 1981 University of Pennsylvania Press edition, based on the original typescript, that Dreiser's original, and much longer, text was published. However, as Dreiser never expressed desire to publish the unedited version of the novel during his lifetime, and as the two versions are not nearly as radically different as might be expected, the debate over which edition closest resembles Dreiser's own wishes for the novel has been going on for almost thirty years. Believing the two versions to be sufficiently similar for the present purposes, with the exception of the chapter titles missing from the 1981 edition, this discussion will rely on the first edition of 1900, which is also the basis of the authoritative Norton Critical Edition edited by Donald Pizer. For a brief but more than adequate discussion of the issues and circumstances associated with the two editions, see Pizer, *The Theory and Practice of American Literary Naturalism* (1993), chapter 10, which also has helpful and

When Caroline Meeber boarded the afternoon train for Chicago, her total outfit consisted of a small trunk, a cheap imitation alligator-skin satchel, a small lunch in a paper box, and a yellow leather snap purse, containing her ticket, a scrap of paper containing her sister's address in Van Buren Street, and four dollars in money. It was in August, 1889. She was eighteen years of age, bright, timid, and full of the illusions of ignorance and youth (1).[64]

Resembling Dreiser's own trip to Chicago, Carrie's experience is representative of so many Midwestern small-town men and women going to the city on what Carl S. Smith has called a "one-way ride from the past into the future" (116). The whole passage somehow manages to exclude the possibility of her ever returning home again despite the narrator's deliberately hollow assurance, a few sentences later, that "Columbia City was not so very far away, even once she was in Chicago. What, pray, is a few hours—a few hundred miles?" (1). The attention to her meager belongings indicates that the novel's main characters, in keeping with city values, will be introduced and defined in terms of their clothes, material possessions, and general ability to spend money. "When a girl leaves her home at eighteen," the narration continues, "she does one of two things. Either she falls into saving hands and becomes better, or she rapidly assumes the cosmopolitan standard of virtue and becomes worse. Of an intermediate balance, under the circumstances, there is no possibility" (1). Carrie soon has her first encounter with the big city in the shape of the salesman Drouet, who, with his rings, gold buttons and "[g]ood clothes […] without which he was nothing" (3), leans over to whisper words of promise and temptation. Here, Chicago, the railroad and Drouet form an elaborate metaphor for the tempting city with, as literary critic Harold Kaplan has termed it, the "promise of satisfied

related discussions of self-censorship in Frank Norris's *McTeague* and Stephen Crane's *The Red Badge of Courage*.

64   It is interesting to note that Dreiser set the opening of the novel in 1889, the year he was himself eighteen years old.

desire" (85) ingrained in its countless arms and agents reaching out into the country looking for young girls to corrupt. Dreiser's naturalistic city begins where the railroad ends, and the inevitable "downfall" of Carrie begins with her decision to board the afternoon train.

After some time, Carrie becomes "conscious of an inequality" between herself and Drouet, based solely on a comparison between his flashy appearance and her own "plain blue dress" and the "worn state of her shoes" (4). Drouet soon uses his worldly advantage and convinces Carrie to surrender her sister's address in the city—with whom she is going to stay—and as the train approaches the city, as night is symbolically falling, Carrie's thoughts are generalized by Dreiser into a statement made by every hopeful newcomer to the magical glimmering city: "Says the soul of the toiler to itself, 'I shall soon be free. I shall be in the ways and the hosts of the merry. The streets, the lamps, the lighted chamber set for dining, are for me. The theater, the halls, the parties, the ways of rest and the paths of song—these are mine in the night" (7). Here the city represents opportunities for material consumption and upper class leisure, illusions that are all banished by the "cold reality" of her sister's "perfunctory embrace," and the chapter ends with a metaphorical picture of Carrie alone "in a tossing, thoughtless sea" (8). In this introductory chapter, Dreiser sets up the naturalistic dominoes for the rest of the novel and almost excludes the possibility of Carrie following another course than letting herself fall into the hands of Drouet. Later, when he proves of little economic importance, she attaches herself to the upscale saloon manager Hurstwood and exchanges sex for material favors in three cities before the novel ends with her as a successful actress on the New York stage.

At first, however, Carrie is just another wage-seeker in a city with a "high and mighty air calculated to overawe and abash the common applicant" (13), and where the department stores display "nothing which she did not long to own" (18). When she applies for a job in a sweatshop, the foreman looks her over "as one would a package" (20), and it is only when Carrie is on the brink of giving up and ready to admit her failure to conquer the city that Drouet almost demonically reappears, takes her out to dinner and lends her money, again whetting her appetite for city life. Drouet, however, as an individual, is not necessarily a bad or immoral man, and neither, to be sure, is Hurstwood. Instead, along with Carrie herself and almost everybody else in the city, both of them are acting under the influence of "forces wholly superhuman [...] [whose] beauty, like music, too often relaxes, then weakens, then perverts the simpler human perceptions" (2). Dreiser never fully explains the exact nature of these superhuman forces, but the novel suggests that the "hypnotic influence" (65) of modern Chicago—a city where attention to traditional values has been replaced with "[a] blare of sound, a roar of life, a vast array of human hives" (2)—numbs the senses and requires of its inhabitants more power of resistance than Carrie, with her "average little conscience," is able to muster (75). In a world where the ten-dollar bills are "soft and noiseless" (49), and where her understanding of money extends to "something everybody else has and I must get" (51), the trap has been set long before Carrie arrives in Chicago.

Dreiser's vision of the world, despite his fondness for the supernatural, is that of a scientist, and in *Sister Carrie* the streets, parks, saloons and apartments of Chicago, and later New York, are the laboratory in which his experiments unfold. Placing his morally ambiguous characters in a world of forces utterly incomprehensible and beyond individual control, he explores what literary historian Warner Berthoff has called "[t]he extraordinary looseness of social relationships, the mobility of position and status, the corresponding insecurity of personal existence" (239). In a modern city founded on the principles of capitalism and social Darwinism, money, status and morals are impermanent entities, and all of the major characters— Carrie, Drouet, Hurstwood and his wife—are on several occasions seen sitting in rocking chairs as if they were unstable atoms fluctuating between failure and success.[65] Further expanding on this theme

---

65 The consistency of this image is impossible to ignore. The characters are mentioned as occupying a rocking chair, or simply as "rocking" in one no less

is Dreiser's insistence on presenting society as a world of a stable amount of energy, transferred but never exhausted, in such a way that the eventual fall of Hurstwood into unemployment and, finally, his suicide conversely mirrors the impressive rise of Carrie, while Drouet acts simply as a catalyst for exchange between the two poles and therefore sees his fortunes largely unaffected. As an effect of the social experiments that the always somber Dreiser presents throughout these pages, the novel seems to be following the only course open to its characters and progresses steadfastly toward its inevitable conclusion. Therefore, the moral undoing of Carrie becomes less a failure on her part to remain virtuous than an unfortunate but natural outcome of the circumstances in which she finds herself.

His career as a novelist delayed for more than a decade by the commercial failure of *Sister Carrie*, Dreiser was to write several other long narratives set either wholly or partly in Chicago. But while all of them recycled and expanded upon his vision of the city, none of them approached *Sister Carrie* in clarity of purpose and unity of theme.[66] Dreiser's prose grew gaudier over time, as in the opening pages of *The Titan*, the middle volume of his "Trilogy of Desire," published in 1914, about the financier Frank Cowperwood:

> To whom may the laurels of this Florence of the West yet fall? This singing flame of a city, this all America, this poet in chaps and buckskin, this rude, raw Titan, this Burns of a city! By its shimmering lake it lay, a king of shreds and patches, a maundering yokel with an epic in its mouth, a tramp, a hobo among cities, with the grip of Cæsar in its mind, the dramatic force of Euripides in its soul. A very bard of a city this, singing of high deeds and high hopes,

than twenty-four times during the novel, the motif being applied most persistently to Carrie (thirteen times) and Hurstwood (eight times).

66   *Sister Carrie*, despite the edits made before its publication, sold less than seven hundred copies, and it was not until the unexpected success of the novel upon publication in Britain, several years later, that Dreiser recommenced to write fiction.

its heavy brogans buried deep in the mire of circumstance. Take Athens, oh, Greece! Italy, do you keep Rome! This was the Babylon, the Troy, the Nineveh of a younger day. Here came the gaping West and the hopeful East to see. Here hungry men, raw from the shops and fields, idyls and romances in their minds, builded them an empire crying glory in the mud (6).

In this rapturous cascade of exclamation points and purple prose, both of which are typical of his later works, Dreiser manages to convey some of the excitement he felt for Chicago, but he does so at the expense of the coherent and concise vision of the city he presented in *Sister Carrie*. Important parts of *Jennie Gerhardt*, *The Financier*, *The Stoic*, *The "Genius"* and *An American Tragedy* also take place in Chicago, but Dreiser's definitive statement about the inescapable dwarfing of the human will in this—America's most modern city, in which everyone is victimized by the desires instigated by a society never willing to fulfill its promise—remains that of his first novel.[67] A masterful work of Chicago fiction, *Sister Carrie* was instrumental in taking American literature from the genteel tradition into the modern world of consumerism and the primitive powers of uncontrolled capitalism.

---

67   Especially in *The "Genius"* does Dreiser once again suggest the boundless joy and opportunities offered by Chicago: "There were great banks, great office buildings, great retail stores, great hotels. The section was running with a tide of people which represented the youth, the illusions, the untrained aspirations, of millions of souls. When you walked into this area you could feel what Chicago meant—eagerness, hope, desire. It was a city that put vitality into almost every wavering heart: it made the beginner dream dreams; the aged to feel that misfortune was never so grim that it might not change" (39). To the experienced reader of Dreiser, however, this passage—like the one quoted above from *The Titan* and so many others just like it—finally collapses under the weight of Dreiser's prose and his excessive fondness for repetition.

The Newspaper Phenomenon and the
Middle Class City of Regular People

While the main current of Chicago literature in the years around the turn of the century concerned itself with the city's businessmen and leading citizens, another kind of literary expression examining other segments of society simultaneously came into being. Chicago was a quickly growing city in almost constant flux. This presented new realities to be described and interpreted almost every day to a diverse population largely unaccustomed to urban living. Therefore, when innovative Chicago newspaper editors and publishers decided to aim for a larger circulation and supplemented commercial and political news with items of a more general interest, they struck fertile ground and enlarged, as Bernard Duffey has said, the Chicago newspaper from "a tool of narrow utility to one of the broadest possible appeal" (10). With this breakthrough, based on legendary *Daily News* founder Melville E. Stone's assertion that "[u]nlike our competitors we must with single-mindedness accept as our only master, our readers" (quoted in Duffey, 11), Chicago became the birthplace of the modern American popular newspaper. At the time of the World's Columbian Exposition there were at least twenty-seven active dailies in the city, catering to virtually all segments of the public.[68]

Essential to the attempt to create a loyal readership in an increasingly diverse city was the humorous columnist who, if successful, could establish a certain continuity in an ephemeral medium destined for the wastebasket within hours of its publication. The most popular of these columnists, Eugene Field, George Ade and Finley Peter Dunne, combined literary ambition with mass appeal and understood, as critic Janet St. Clair has argued, that "Chicago must shape a character all its own from a unification of its own disparate elements" (238). They created a truly democratic literature by giving

---

68   The number of daily newspapers has been determined by Gilbert, 48. For an exhaustive list of Chicago periodicals until 1893, see the impressive appendices in Kenny J. Williams, *Prairie Voices* (1980).

voice to the concerns of an ever-increasing middle class population of clerks and shop-girls who now, for the first time, could feel included in the social life of the sprawling metropolis.[69]

Eugene Field

Perhaps no one writing in Chicago during the last two decades of the nineteenth century was more preoccupied with the social pretensions of the city's upper classes than Eugene Field. From 1883 until his early death in 1895, Field wrote a column in the *Daily News* entitled "Sharps and Flats." Born in St. Louis in 1850 and educated in the East, he was lured to Chicago from Denver, where he was managing editor of the local *Tribune*. A romantic at heart, he was daily confronted with the commercial realities of "Porkopolis," as he liked to call it, and many of his best columns from the early years, collected in 1887 as *Culture's Garland*, were directed at "the refined taste of the *élite* of Chicago" (153), who "do not know what an eroica symphony is; but

---

69   Finley Peter Dunne, while not discussed in the following, was nevertheless an important figure among the Chicago newspaper columnists. His recurring character Mr. Dooley, a saloon-keeper in the city's Irish Catholic working class Bridgeport neighborhood, offered a mildly satiric comment on city events and other issues in the *Evening Post*, written in a pioneering use of dialect. His take on original sin is a typical example: "'Twas took out iv me be Father Tuomy with holy water first an' be me father aftherward with a sthrap" (161). Due to the largely contemporary nature of his subject matter, however, much of Dunne's satire is hard to grasp today without an intimate knowledge of turn-of-the-century Chicago politics and history, and most critical works dealing with his sketches go to great lengths to put them in context. Dunne was for several years in the late 1890s probably the most popular of the city's famous columnists, and after the Spanish-American War of 1898, and with the advent of newspaper syndication, Mr. Dooley became a national phenomenon, pouring out equal amounts of beer and unconventional Irish wisdom until World War I. Probably the best critical work contextualizing Dunne is Edward J. Bander, *Mr. Dooley and Mr. Dunne: The Literary Life of a Chicago Catholic* (1981).

in our most cultured circles, it is believed that eroica is a misprint for erotica" (154).[70]

Often using the pose of an earnest recorder of cultural activity in the city, Field mentions many of the most prominent citizens, showing little or no restraint in his lampooning of such figures as Potter Palmer and George Pullman. In a series of columns, Field imagines that Pullman, after having furnished "King Humbert of Italy" (51) with a Pullman Palace Car, has been offered the choice between the title of marchese or chevalier, but, as the reporter notes, "we are inclined to think that markeesy sounds just a trifle more bong tong than sheevalya, and we hope that Mr. Pullman will choose that title" (54). Next, Field designs and prints a coat of arms for Pullman, featuring two Pullman porters holding a pillow with a bedbug on it and the motto "Pro Patria Cavaliere," the beauty of which is that "it can be abridged to P. P. C., and thus be made to serve a business purpose" (56). Chicago society responds to the news in different ways, Field explains, and while the Italian minority rejoices and introduces the "macaroni di Pullman" (58) on restaurant menus, a local poet jealously composes the following song, which showcases Field's particular talent for light verse:

> When the party is breezy and wheezy,
> And palpably greasy, it's easy
>> To coax or to wring,
>> From a weak-minded king,
> The titular prize of markeesy (64).

Field was a master of this particular brand of nonsense, piling joke upon joke on a relatively slight initial idea, and one can be sure that he made the self-styled Chicago aristocracy open their morning paper with trepidation, fearing that their turn had come to be ridiculed

---

70 The garland of the title appears as a drawing on the flyleaves, bearing the inscription "A Chicago Literary Circle: In the Similitude of a Laurel Wreath" and is made entirely of linked sausages.

before the entire city by his peculiar wit and uncensored personal attacks.

What Field saw in Chicago was an essentially materialistic city desperately trying to buy cultural respectability, and he wrote many fictional stories of prominent citizens betraying their ignorance, for example by paying fortunes for "an autograph of Dante Alighieri [...] discovered on the fly-leaf of a volume of Ella Wheeler Wilcox's poems" (58). He also enjoyed describing how "the *crème de la crème* of our *élite* lift up their hands, and groan, when they discover that it takes as long to play a classical symphony as it does to slaughter a carload of Missouri razor-backs, or an invoice of prairie-racers from Kansas" (149). As Kenny J. Williams has observed, Field believed that the "cultural unawareness in the city was matched only by a total lack of taste and literary acumen" (1974, 92), and he later became involved in the running controversy surrounding the new literary style of realism. In a series of columns aimed at Hamlin Garland, who, he said, had fallen under "the baleful influence of William Dean Howells," Field aligned himself with the romanticists and said about Garland's work that "it is wonderful photography" (1901, 49).[71]

Especially in his later—and somewhat tamer—newspaper columns, Field presented himself as being of a fundamentally romantic nature, believing, as he wrote, "in ghosts, in witches, and in fairies [...] I adore dolls" (1969, 128). It is therefore no surprise that his only novel, an unfinished volume entitled *The House*, published posthumously in 1896, has as its central theme the opposition between astronomer Reuben Baker, an incurable romantic, and his pragmatic wife Alice. The couple have dreamt of owning a house throughout their twenty years of marriage, and while Reuben is satisfied to keep dreaming of "a palatial residence with a dance-hall at the top and a

---

71 As with his reaction to Henry B. Fuller's "The Downfall of Abner Joyce," the jovial Garland seems to have taken no offense by the comments made by Field. In *Roadside Meetings* (1930) he dismisses the controversy as a friendly "local skirmish" (252) and notes that by 1893, the year Field made the comments, "Eugene and I had already become something more than acquaintances" (241).

wine-cellar at the bottom" (2), Alice one day surprisingly announces that she has bought an old farmhouse on Chicago's North Side. After a promising beginning, the novel turns into a humorously told but slightly pedestrian description of the various problems encountered by Chicago homeowners. The couple are soon dealing with plumbers, painters and city ordinances regarding the watering of lawns, as well as fighting off the numerous salesmen soon appearing from enterprises such as "the Royal Liliuokalani Fire, Marine and Accident Insurance Company of Hawaii" (156), under whose "soothing balm bereavement becomes an actual pleasure" (183). The running joke is that the naïve and good-natured dreamer Reuben is persuaded time and again to invest in ludicrous schemes, while Alice's more realistic disposition, along with her fondness for action, is of little help. The central opposition remains largely unexplored, however, and the novel desperately lacks the satiric wit of Field's newspaper columns.[72] *The House* offers instead a rare middle class version of Chicago, and because the biggest dramas unfold when the couple choose their hardware fixtures or when the gas company tears up the lawn to lay pipes, the novel is a reminder that Chicago was not exclusively inhabited by grain-speculators and crooked businessmen, but was also a city of a growing middle class.

Field himself remains something of an enigma. Famous in Chicago for his satiric sketches, he preferred to be associated with his lighter verse and was often referred to as "the children's poet," because he wrote such overtly sentimental rhymes as "Little Boy Blue" and "Wynken, Blynken, and Nod," which turned him into a national sensation. A contemporary article in the *Overland Monthly* laments

---

72   Running out of ideas near the end, an uninspired Field summons the always reliable Hamlin Garland, or "Gamlin Harland" as he is called, who, as is by now to be expected, proceeds to prophesize that the new responsibilities associated with the house "will take your mind off your impracticable star-gazing and moonshining, and divert your attention into the channels of realism … You can now lay aside the telescope and the spectrum for the spade and the hoe; the field of speculation can be abandoned for this noble acre" (186).

his death as a "national loss" ("Eugene Field's Death," 672) and calls him "the only really great western writer" (672), focusing exclusively on his fairytales and children's poems which are compared to those of Hans Christian Andersen and Louisa May Alcott. In a historical perspective, however, it is clear that Field's major accomplishment is his columns which, as critic Robert A. Day has argued, "furnishes a commentary on one phase of America's cultural development, and gives a detailed picture of the hobbledehoy age of Chicago" (478)—a picture that because of its unusual perspective on Chicago life is his most lasting contribution to literature.

George Ade

Of the Chicago newspaper columnists of the 1890s, it was perhaps George Ade who made best use of the new city reality as a unique location for literature. Ade was born in small-town Indiana in 1866, and after graduating from Purdue University he worked as a reporter for the Lafayette *Call* before making his way to Chicago in 1890. Starting out with a daily piece on the weather, Ade soon became a feature writer and eventually landed his own column in the *Record*, the morning edition of the *Daily News*—which carried Eugene Field's clever sketches. Between 1893 and 1900, the column appeared anonymously on the editorial page as "Stories of the Streets and of the Town," and in it Ade gave daily voice and identity to various characters from all layers of society, both in and out of the mainstream, and revealed in this way, from a decidedly middle class perspective, the city to its own inhabitants.

Ade had a good eye for colorful detail, and during his first years in the city the column often consisted of simple and sentimental descriptions of certain streets or city features, such as "The Junk-Shops of Canal Street" and "Vehicles Out of the Ordinary," both of which celebrate the variety of the Chicago experience. The former describes the "tottering, aged and unpainted little structures" of Canal Street (*Chicago Stories*, 80) where "everything is picturesquely dull and smoke stained" (83), while the latter concerns itself with a number of unusual wagons found in the city, ranging from the "old cobbler and his traveling shop" (88) to a sandwich car where, "[i]f one is not troubled with a false pride one can get a good warm lunch at low prices and stand on the curbstone while he eats it" (89). Another sketch reminisces about "Old Days on the Canal," and Ade seems surprisingly unhindered by the fact that he had been in the city for only a few years, describing as he does Chicago "before the town lay under a pall of smoke and the rushing trains bore down their victims at every crossing" (51).

Perhaps the most telling of these early descriptive sketches is one entitled "The Advantage of Being 'Middle Class,'" in which, as historian James Gilbert has noted, Ade shows that "it is acceptable, even exciting, to participate in the popular culture of the city and, despite all appearances, there is nothing at all immoral about this culture" (50). In the column, Ade plays once again the role of the detached outsider, observing and reporting events as he makes his way around the city, all the while arguing that "the middle class has a monopoly of the real enjoyment in Chicago" as they are not "held down by the arbitrary laws governing that mysterious part of the community known as society" (75). The Chicago middle class, Ade says, can enjoy such free or cheap entertainments as summer-night boat trips on the lake, street orchestras, and strolls in the parks on warm evenings. In addition, he notes, middle class families buying ice cream often "send one of the children with a pitcher. If they were above the middle class, of course, it would never do for them to be seen in a common ice-cream place, and the idea of sending a pitcher would be shocking" (75). Ade's column was written predominantly for the growing middle class of clerks and shop girls, and the purpose of the sketches was simply to cajole and flatter readers into believing that theirs was the best of all worlds, and that they should "feel sorry for the millionaire, who cannot go to a public park in the evening to stroll or sit for the reasons that so many other persons go there. It doesn't trouble the delivery boy to have other people present and enjoying themselves" (79). Characteristic of his literary project, Ade rarely mentions the lower classes—those who do not possess the means for enjoying a boat trip on the lake—and when he does, it is in ways and terms strictly belonging to his familiar middle class perspective, such as his stereotypic description of the "Clark Street Chinamen" or the fable-like circumstances of "'Hobo' Wilson and the Good Fairy." His is a safe version of Chicago where illicit behavior and the dangers feared by the middle class are seen at a distance or given a slight spin, such as when the couple holding hands on the park-bench turn out to be married, or when the girl in the window across the street is suddenly holding a baby with hair as red as the policeman who occasionally visits her.[73]

As he progressed with the column, Ade became increasingly in-terested in longer narrative and began constructing sketches with recurring characters, with each new column adding a little to an on-going story or general characterization. Two of these recognizable Chicago types, Artie Blanchard and Pink Marsh, had their sketches collected and published as the "novels" *Artie* and *Pink Marsh* in 1896 and 1897, and represent Ade at the top of his creative powers.[74] The ubiquitous William Dean Howells probably had *Artie* in mind when he commented that "in Mr. George Ade the American spirit arrives: arrives, puts down its grip, looks around, takes a chair and makes itself at home. It has no questions to ask and none to answer" (1903, 739). The novel is a good example of the unmistakably modern Chicago young man who works a white-collar job in a tall office building—he is a "clerk"—and defines himself and his surroundings largely by the use of argot and big-city manners and values.

Artie, as he says himself, knows the city "like a book" (84), and the novel follows him for roughly a year, in which he goes from being

---

73 Occurring, respectively, in "The Advantage of Being 'Middle Class'" and "From the Office Window."

74 Another character whose sketches were collected in a "novel" was the affable old gentleman Doc Horne, who lived in the decaying Alfalfa European Hotel and spent his time telling fantastic stories of his youth to the other resi-dents. The sketches were collected in a 1899 book which, while certainly enter-taining, is of significantly less interest for the present purposes than *Artie* and *Pink Marsh*, as it adds little to the Chicago perspective of Ade's work.

a fast-talking wise-cracker who has seen it all and who frequently shows up for work with a hangover and a wild story of the night before to a slightly more mature version of himself as he gradually falls in love with a girl called Mamie. He slowly works up the courage to pop the question, which he does in the final sketch, where he is surprisingly sincere as he tries to prove that "I ain't as foolish sometimes as I am others" (107). Artie is a good example of who Ade had in mind when he described the numerous advantages of being middle class. Working in a skyscraper, Artie is already immersed in the promise of upward social movement that Fuller's Cornelia McNabb felt so intensely upon entering the Clifton, and his relatively well-paid and respectable job allows him the opportunity of a bachelor lifestyle of some leisure, making it possible for him to take his "girlerino" (39) on the kind of boat rides and park strolls Ade championed in the descriptive sketches. In order to make Artie as realistic as possible, Ade wrote the dialogue in the new urban vernacular he observed on the streets and in the offices around town, where young middle class men invented a particular slang fitted to the age and their place in society. Artie, therefore, mostly because of his verbal shenanigans, fascinates his less experienced co-workers when he tells them about a poker game of last night in the following manner: "I stands pat on the draw, and then the first crack out o' the box I whoops it a half—fifty kopecks. What does he do? He could n't drop his hand too quick. Another case o' licked in a punch" (13). With *Artie*, Ade sharply defined a character so recognizable from contemporary life and yet so foreign to literature that it made Howells marvel at the novelty of the material and remark that "[y]ou are not asked to be interested in any one because he is in any way out of the common, but because he is in every way in the common" (1903, 740).

Another of Ade's recurring characters, a type familiar to most but largely ignored in life as well as in literature, was the eponymous black shoeshine boy of the collection of sketches published as *Pink Marsh*. Where Artie worked in a tall office building and had hopes of one day reaching the top, Pink finds himself in a barbershop below street-level and dreams of working at the racetracks. Most of the sketches take the form of a conversation between Pink and the regular "morning customer," with Pink providing a simple and sometimes unconventional perspective on such topics as the origin of the species and whether or not to believe what the Bible says: "I do n' know what all's in 'at Bible, but I say it's so, o' else it would n't be in. I'm takin' no chances, misteh. I ain' no good chuhch membeh now, but I'm goin' o' keep good on believin' in 'at Bible, so if eveh I get sick o' anything 'e matteh 'ith me, I wont have to squaih myse'f ve'y much" (201). Stereotyped though he is, Pink nevertheless appears as a real character and a distinct individual, and he eventually gives up drinking and gets a job as a railway porter before the story ends, much to the delight of the morning customer who takes an almost fatherly interest in the young man.

In *Artie* and *Pink Marsh*, Ade brought his middle class humanity and infallible ear for dialect to two completely different characters, and he created in the process two pioneering works of Chicago realism. In later years, however, as he began to experiment with his famous "Fables in Slang," which were widely syndicated and brought him sometimes as much as $2,500 a story, he abandoned realism almost completely and became instead, as Bernard Duffey has regretted, the nation's "master gag-writer" (21).[75] Some of the fables are amusing, if unremarkable. One of the more successful, "The Fable of the Old Fox and the Young Fox," contains several nuggets of useful advice from the older to the younger generation, the turning of conventional wisdom on its head being a favorite of the later Ade's mild humor: "Early to Bed and Early to Rise is a Bad Rule for any one who wishes to become acquainted with our most Prominent and Influential People" (1947, 113). Having turned his attention away from

---

75 The amount received by Ade for a story is reported by John T. McCutcheon, Ade's lifelong friend and illustrator of many of his stories during his Chicago newspaper years, and appears in a letter quoted by Franklin J. Meine in his introduction to a collection of Ade's *Chicago Stories* (1963), xix. So great was the success of the fables that close to one hundred of them were made into short movies between 1914 and 1917.

Chicago, Ade continued churning out fables while simultaneously pursuing a career as a playwright on Broadway, where he enjoyed great success with such musical comedies as *The Sultan of Sulu* and *Peggy from Paris*. His main artistic achievement, however, remains the early columns appearing in "Stories of the Streets and of the Town," which added, along with Eugene Field's *The House*, a realistic middle class perspective to the developing Chicago literature.

Life in the Slums and the Dark Side of Chicago

While Chicago at the turn of the century was certainly home to both grain-speculating millionaires and an emerging and relatively large middle class, it remained for many a city of immense social problems, populated by a lower class consisting mostly of immigrants attracted by the promise of American life. For many, however, this dream had proven to be largely illusory. Differences between rich and poor were perhaps even more explicit in the cities of America than they had been in the Old World, and nowhere was this more transparently obvious than in Chicago, a city with a penchant for exaggeration.

Just as Chicago millionaires were among the richest in the nation and their houses the most splendid, so were the city's slums of such an abominable nature that they became notorious examples of urban development gone dreadfully wrong, causing muckraking journalist Lincoln Steffens, in 1904, to proclaim the city to be "[f]irst in violence, deepest in dirt; loud, lawless, unlovely, ill-smelling, irreverent, new; an overgrown gawk of a village, the 'tough' among cities" (234). With a population of almost two million, the city lacked sufficient political regulation to accommodate and protect its many new citizens, and the sheer number of wage seekers competing for jobs made it easy for employers to exploit the mostly unorganized workers, who were consequently forced to huddle together in slums often unfit for human habitation.

The deplorable conditions endured by Chicago's immigrant proletariat naturally elicited a wide array of different responses, in life as well as in literature, as writers discovered the power of the written word to focus attention on the ever-widening gap between wealth and poverty in the young city.

Jane Addams

Without a doubt the best-known Chicago reformer who successfully fused an intellectual approach to the city's evils with a career as an activist was Jane Addams, who was born in a small northern Illinois town in 1860. After obtaining a degree from Rockford Seminary, she enrolled in a medical college—still unconventional for a woman in the 1880s. But when illness compelled her to give up her studies, she instead went to Europe where she visited, among other places, the famous Toynbee Hall settlement in the East End of London. Inspired to bring the settlement movement to America, Addams returned to Chicago with her friend Ellen Starr and, through the generosity of several benefactors, they established Hull-House on Halsted Street in 1889 and opened, as Henry Steele Commager has phrased it, "its doors to those who cared to enter."[76]

Reminiscing about her experiences in the book *Twenty Years at Hull-House* (1910)—which is the story of the settlement—Addams took stock of the preceding two decades. The book is an interesting account of the development of her social philosophy and the rise of Hull-House from upstart poorhouse, and what Addams liked to think of as a "Cathedral of Humanity" (99), to one of the leading liberal institutions in Chicago. Calling the settlement "an experimental effort to aid in the solution of the social and industrial problems which are engendered by the modern conditions of life in a great city" (83), Addams believed that "education and recreation ought to be extended to the immigrants" (99), and therefore dedicated herself particularly to helping and integrating the countless uprooted and alienated foreigners constituting the extreme lower classes of the city.

---

76   In Henry Steele Commager's foreword to the 1961 Signet Classics edition of Jane Addams's *Twenty Years at Hull-House* (1910), xi.

The book abounds in horrific stories of child labor, infant death, old crippled women, and single mothers of twelve, but it is also the story of the human spirit triumphing over the city's evils as the settlement provides an ever-widening range of artistic and intellectual activities for the sometimes well-educated but largely dispirited immigrants. One of these, Addams recollects, "expressed great surprise when he found that we, although Americans, still liked pictures, and said quite naïvely that he didn't know that Americans cared for anything but dollars—that looking at pictures was something people only did in Italy" (243). For Addams, the challenge of Hull-House was to help make the new Americans realize their human potential and become productive members of society, a task proving difficult when practiced among the intense human misery of a city ruled by "an industry totally unregulated by well-considered legislation" (130) and suffering from a "lack of political machinery adapted to modern city life" (192).

As Hull-House expanded and added new buildings and activities, it became a national phenomenon upon which settlements in the nation's other great cities were modeled, and it came closer to fulfilling the ambition laid out in the charter: "[t]o provide a center for a higher civic and social life; to institute and maintain educational and philanthropic enterprises, and to investigate and improve the conditions in the industrial districts of Chicago" (73).[77] More than two thousand visitors were soon visiting Hull-House daily, and Addams and her co-workers had succeeded in creating an oasis of culture,

---

77 Perhaps the most famous of the cultural activities offered by Hull-House were the University Extension lectures, which became popular with people from all layers of society and attracted speakers on many subjects, such as, for example, the Russian social reformer and anarchist Peter Kropotkin and American educational philosopher John Dewey. That Hull-House had become a Chicago institution is testified to by its frequent mention in the literature of the time, most prominently by Henry B. Fuller (*With the Procession*, 124) and Robert Herrick (*The Common Lot*, 144), both of whom, along with writers such as Edgar Lee Masters, Floyd Dell and Vachel Lindsay, were frequent visitors to the settlement.

help and friendliness in the middle of a socially barren environment of almost unlimited grief and despair. *Twenty Years at Hull-House* stands today as a monument to a few women's devotion to a cause they never ceased to believe in, however desperate the circumstances surrounding them.[78]

Upton Sinclair

For Upton Sinclair, desperate circumstances were an integral part of both his own life and his perception of American society in general. Born in 1878 and brought up in the Baltimore slums with an alcoholic father, Sinclair became a socialist early in life and was, as critic Van Wyck Brooks has concisely said, "convinced that society is ruled by organized greed" (379). This realization prompted him to write muck-raking articles for such magazines as the *Appeal to Reason*, exposing the ways in which big money capitalism exploited the lower classes. When asked to write about the evils of wage slavery, Sinclair went to Chicago's Packingtown district, home to more than a quarter of a million people, and spent almost two months gathering material for what was to be published in 1906 as the sensational and fierce novel *The Jungle*.

Perhaps intended to take advantage of the controversy surrounding a 1904 article in the New York *Independent* by Antanas Kaztauskis, entitled "From Lithuania to the Chicago Stockyards— An Autobiography," the novel follows a Lithuanian family as they arrive in Chicago.[79] The name of the city is the only English word they

---

78 The story of Hull-House was continued by Addams in *The Second Twenty Years at Hull-House* (1930), which is also the story of her presidency of the Women's International League for Peace and Freedom, earning her the Nobel Peace Prize in 1931.

79 The story, told to journalist Ernest Poole (who later won the Pulitzer Prize), recounts in the first person the hardships encountered by a Lithuanian immigrant in the Chicago stockyards as he discovers the American way of life: "That first night we sat around in the house and they asked me, 'Well, why did you come?' I told them about that first night and what the ugly shoemaker said about 'life, liberty and the getting of happiness.' They all leaned back and

know, having probably learned it from the agents of the meatpackers sent to their village for recruitment. Here, what Sinclair perceives as the ruthless man-made forces of the stockyards and the inhuman conditions of the slums first destroy their spirits and later their bodies. The novel opens with the joyful wedding of Jurgis and Ona, occurring after they have been in Chicago for a while, but celebrated according to Lithuanian custom. This strategy allows Sinclair to describe the lively and vital European spirits of the new immigrants. The novel proceeds from there to systematically chronicle the destruction of every last one of their hopes and dreams under the crushing reality of life in the Chicago slums of Packingtown. Soon after arriving, Jurgis goes to the stockyards looking for work. Still young and strong, he is picked among the hundreds of men hopefully waiting outside the gates, landing a job sweeping up entrails in the killing beds, and earning, the narrator ironizes, "the fabulous sum of seventeen and a half cents an hour" (53). Once on the inside, Jurgis's early conception of the stockyards as "a wonderful poem [...] a picture of human power wonderful to watch [...] a thing as tremendous as the universe" (47–51 passim) is radically altered, and he begins to understand the true nature of the place. Carl S. Smith has suggested that "Sinclair uses the stockyards to show how much unnatural and malignant elements have replaced the natural landscape in the modern city" (166), and as Jurgis and his family make their way around the killing beds and other jobs, serving, Sinclair writes, "as cogs in the great packing machine" (96), there is indeed very little to be found that could be

---

laughed. 'What you need is money,' they said. 'It was all right at home. You wanted nothing. You ate your own meat and your own things on the farm. You made your own clothes and had your own leather. The other things you got at the Jew man's store and paid him with sacks of rye. But here you want a hundred things. Whenever you walk out you see new things you want, and you must have money to buy everything'" (245). The story is reminiscent of Sinclair's novel in many aspects, as Kaztauskis arrives in Chicago, is exploited by the meatpackers, and in the end is saved by joining a labor union, suggesting both a very common experience, and one doctored perhaps by Poole to fit the purposes of his political agenda, just as with the polemical *The Jungle*.

classified as nature.[80] The entirety of the stockyards resembles one gigantic machine, taking in live animals in one end and pushing out hundreds of finished products at the other, wasting nothing in the process as even the bones and excrement of the livestock are used to make fertilizer in a section seldom accessed by visitors, while "the few who did would come out looking like Dante, of whom the peasants declared that he had been into hell" (154). In the Chicago stockyards, the butcher of old has been displaced by industrial machinery, and just as the downtown skyscrapers serve as metaphors for the possibility of upward social mobility in the novels of Henry B. Fuller and Robert Herrick, so do the horrid working conditions of the stockyards, along with their surrounding slums, represent in Sinclair's novel a static social position and a virtual hell filled with "black volcanoes of smoke" (210).

Throughout, Sinclair's strategy consists of first presenting the reader with glimmers of budding hope. These include Jurgis getting a job on his first day, the family buying a house on the installment plan, and Ona giving birth to a son. Sinclair then lets a compound of the corrupt city, the indifferent society and the exploiting meatpackers, often referred to with an impersonal "them" or "they," strike repeatedly by having Jurgis fired without good reason and his house taken away as a consequence of failed payments. The ultimate blow arrives when little Antanas, who represents "the one delight that Jurgis had in the world" (250), drowns in the foul-smelling waters of the unpaved roads of Packingtown. Such are the miseries of the extended

---

80   A good example of the unremitting routine expected of the immigrant worker can be found in a pamphlet distributed among Polish laborers of Chicagoan Cyrus Hall McCormick's International Harvester Corporation and designed to teach them English: "Lesson One. I hear the whistle. I must hurry. I hear the five minute whistle. It is time to go into the shop. I take my check from the gate board and hang it on the department board. I change my clothes and get ready to work. The starting whistle blows. I eat my lunch. It is forbidden to eat until then. The whistle blows at five minutes of starting time. I get ready to go to work. I work until the whistle blows to quit. I leave my place nice and clean. I put all my clothes in the locker. I must go home" (quoted in Gutman, 6).

family: One member loses his fingers cutting meat, another has his legs and lungs slowly eaten away by the chemicals used in the pickle room, a young boy is eaten alive by rats, and, finally, Ona is forced into prostitution by her boss and later dies in childbirth as the family cannot afford a real doctor.[81] The formerly lively and vital European family thus pays a heavy price in their pursuit of the American dream, and are in the end butchered like hogs in the Darwinian jungle of Chicago's stockyards. "The game had never been fair," the narrator says, and "the dice were loaded" (199).

As the family is destroyed, Jurgis leaves Chicago and goes tramping before being drawn back into the city—like a piece of shrapnel to the magnet—as winter approaches. At this point the novel all but abandons its avowed realism, and turns instead into a vehicle for Sinclair's preaching of the benefits of socialism. Jurgis first becomes involved with the labor unions and later with the socialist party itself. Handed books to read, his uneducated mind slowly begins to understand the motivation of the packers: "What they wanted from a hog was all the profits that could be got out of him; and that was what they wanted from the working man, and also what they wanted from the public" (376). As for the larger-scale Beef Trust operating at the top, Sinclair writes, "[i]t was a monster devouring with a thousand mouths, trampling with a thousand hoofs; it was the Great Butcher—it was the spirit of Capitalism made flesh. Upon the ocean of commerce it sailed as a pirate ship; it had hoisted the black flag and declared war upon civilization" (376–377). Abandoning both nar-

---

81 The novel's endless parade of naturalistic misery elicited the following response from Robert Herrick: "It is done in the Zola manner, that is as Zola is understood in America: every misfortune that might possibly befall workers in the stockyards during the last dozen years is made to visit the luckless hero and his family. And all the filth that might be found in the industry of providing animal food for the millions is spread along the pages. Probably every evil exposed has a germ of truth in it; but the whole is hideous distortion. The result is not literature; it is not fact; it is 'good stuff'" (MS, The University of Chicago Library). Even Herrick, who was otherwise ablaze with hate for American capitalism and accompanying commercialism, found *The Jungle* hard to stomach.

rative and human interest to a rather uninteresting political agenda, the novel's final chapter ultimately fails to live up to the undeniable power of its earlier parts where the melodramatic developments and slightly constructed feel of the narrative had been easily overcome by Sinclair's compassion for the human destinies involved.[82]

In the end, the novel proved to serve the purpose of reform, but did so in an entirely different way than had been expected by Sinclair at the outset. Instead of provoking a public outcry supporting better working conditions for the immigrants of Packingtown and elsewhere, the bestseller directly brought about the Pure Food and Drug Act of 1906, as readers were more outraged by the descriptions of the unsanitary and repulsive circumstances under which their meat products had been prepared than by the bondage of the wage slaves. Sinclair famously commented in his *Autobiography* that "I aimed at the public's heart, and by accident I hit it in the stomach" (126). Despite his disillusionment, however, it can be said about few novels of the time that they hit president Theodore Roosevelt in the stomach and helped to change in a small way a society that was, as Sinclair wrote in *The Jungle*, "from top to bottom [...] nothing but one gigantic lie" (91).

Jack London

Jack London appears in *The Jungle* as the barely masked "young author" (388) who, "because he was a man of genius [...] forced the world to hear him. Now he was famous, but wherever he went he still preached the gospel of the poor" (388). London called the novel "[t]he *Uncle Tom's Cabin* of wage-slavery" and predicted that what Harriet Beecher Stowe's novel had done for black slaves, "*The Jungle*

---

82 The faults of the novel's final chapters were painfully clear to Sinclair himself, as he wrote in his *Autobiography*: "The last chapters were not up to standard, because both my health and my money were gone, and a second trip to Chicago, which I had hoped to make, was out of the question. I did the best I could—and those critics who didn't like the ending ought to have seen it as it was in manuscript!" (114).

has a large chance to do for the white slaves of today."[83] When the novel failed to have the desired effect, London himself wrote a novel describing the evils of capitalism and decided to take the story to what he saw as its logical conclusion. *The Jungle*, after all, had ended with the socialists chanting the words, twice repeated, first in italics and then in full capitals, "CHICAGO WILL BE OURS!" (411). And because London subscribed to the theories of Marxism, there was logically only one way to fulfill that prophecy, and that way was revolution.

The Iron Heel, London's novel chronicling the build-up to a failed American revolution, appeared in 1907. It employs as its central device a pretense to having been written by the wife of Ernest Everhard, the not so subtly named leader of the revolution, who is described as an "intellectual swashbuckler" (18) and "a superman, a blond beast [...] aflame with democracy" (8). Furthering the conceit, the manuscript has supposedly been discovered seven centuries later, in the age of the "Brotherhood of Man" (3), allowing London to step outside his time and comment in the footnotes on contemporary society as if it were some earlier and incomprehensible stage of human development. Reflecting on corruption in the early twentieth century, the future historian characteristically spells out the point for London's readers:

> Even as late as A.D. 1912, the great mass of the people still persisted in the belief that they ruled the country by virtue of their ballots. In reality the country was ruled by what were called *political machines*. At first the machine bosses charged the master capitalists extortionate tolls for legislation; but in a short time the master capitalists found it cheaper to own the political machines themselves and to hire the machine bosses (54n).

---

83   The comment—made by London in a letter originally published in the *Appeal to Reason* and designed to help boost sales of *The Jungle*—is quoted from Sinclair's *My Lifetime in Letters* (1960), 20.

The city of Chicago, while not playing an important part in most of the narrative, has nevertheless, as the contemporary narrator points out, "always been the storm-centre of the conflict between labor and capital, a city of street-battles and violent death, with a class-conscious capitalist organization and a class-conscious workman organization" (197). The city is therefore the natural place for Everhard's revolution to begin its nationwide course.[84] Once the revolutionary wheels have been set in motion, the situation spins out of control as it is discovered that the oligarchy ruling America has been informed of the plans, and the result is therefore scenes of grotesque urban warfare between "the people of the abyss" (159) and the troops of the ruling classes in "that modern jungle, a great city" (204).[85] While the battle was raging, the narrator is later told, the children of the oligarchy played happily in the parks, where "their favourite game was an imitation of their elders stamping upon the proletariat" (213), an image that anticipates the total failure of the revolution and helps

---

84   As the action moves to Chicago, London, in a footnote, mentions real-life English labor leader John Burns's response to a question regarding his opinion of the city: "'Chicago,' he answered, 'is a pocket edition of hell.' Some time later, as he was going aboard his steamer to sail to England, he was approached by another reporter who wanted to know if he had changed his opinion of Chicago. 'Yes, I have,' was his reply. 'My present opinion is that hell is a pocket edition of Chicago'" (196 n).

85   In 1903 London had published *The People of the Abyss*, his account of spending several weeks among the poor of the Whitechapel district of London, into which he went, he writes in the preface, "with an attitude of mind which I may best liken to that of the explorer" (ix). In *The Iron Heel*, he correctly ascribes the coining of the phrase of his title to "the genius of H. G. Wells," but misdates it to "the late nineteenth century A.D." (159 n). Wells first employed the term in his 1902 book of futurologist social theory entitled *Anticipations: Of the Reaction of Mechanical and Scientific Progress Upon Human Life and Thought*, using it to represent one of the four main human categories in an inevitable future human society, the other three being the Efficients, the Speculators, and the Irresponsible Rich.

the reader understand why it was to take seven centuries to reach the present-day "Brotherhood of Man."

The Iron Heel is a very pessimistic novel. While *The Jungle* ended with the hope of socialism on the rise, London's narrator is cut off—and the novel ends—in mid-sentence, as she contemplates another attempt at rebellion: "The magnitude of the task may be understood when it is taken into." And there Jack London's revolution ends. The important part, however, is that a revolution *did* take place, and that it took place in Chicago, "the industrial inferno of the nineteenth century" (196 n), even if it failed to overturn society and bring equality to the workers of the nation. With *The Iron Heel* London continued the logic of *The Jungle* and followed it in presenting the essential helplessness of common man in American society, represented by the overpowering circumstances of the Chicago slums.

While novelists such as Henry B. Fuller and Robert Herrick were busy exploring the commercial nature of Chicago during its formative years, and did so by scrutinizing the empty morals and unethical methods of the city's economic aristocracy, writers and activists such as Jane Addams, Upton Sinclair and Jack London aligned themselves with the people who lacked the intellectual abilities to completely fathom the system that suppressed them. The slums and the lower classes were as integral a part of the Chicago experience as the skyscrapers, the businessmen, and the emerging middle class of the newspaper columnists, and their often desperate circumstances offered the reform writers a condensed version of the bottom of American society that lent itself readily to their literary strategies. With works such as *Twenty Years at Hull-House*, *The Jungle* and *The Iron Heel*, the new American urban proletariat made its appearance in literature.

The Second Generation and the
Chicago Renaissance

Chicago literature had since its imaginative inception following the World's Columbian Exposition tried to define for itself and for society at large the meaning of the new urban experience offered by the growing Midwestern metropolis. America was no longer the same country it had been only a generation earlier, and the national consciousness had become occupied with new ideals and concepts symbolic of the age of industrial capitalism.[86] With the appearance of the businessman as the new cultural hero, and with concepts such as slums and the budding middle class making their way into American life, the first generation of Chicago writers sought to explore the significance of the new realities while crafting for themselves a set of literary conventions that made it possible for them to discover Chicago as a subject for serious literature. Their accomplishments were of a varied and for the most part successful nature, and they helped lay the groundwork for future generations of writers working with mate-

---

86   In *A Traveler from Altruria*, his 1894 utopian novel telling the story of an Altrurian's encounter with modern American society, William Dean Howells offered the following analysis of the changing face of the American ideal: "I should say that within a generation our ideal has changed twice. Before the war, and during all the time from the revolution onward, it was undoubtedly the great politician, the publicist, the statesman. As we grew older and began to have an intellectual life of our own, I think the literary fellows had a pretty good share of the honors that were going; that is, such a man as Longfellow was popularly considered a type of greatness. When the war came, it brought the soldier to the front, and there was a period of ten or fifteen years where he dominated the national imagination. That period passed, and the great era of material prosperity set in. The big fortunes began to tower up, and heroes of another sort began to appeal to our admiration. I don't think there is any doubt but the millionaire is now the American ideal. It isn't very pleasant to think so, even for people who have got on, but it can't be very hopefully denied. It is the man with the most money who now takes the prize in our national cake-walk" (138).

rial native to the city and established a tradition both to build upon and rebel against.

With the second decade of the twentieth century, most of the writers belonging to the first generation were either prematurely dead, like Field and Norris, burned out artistically, like Fuller and Herrick, or had moved on to New York and bigger things, like Garland and Ade. Only Theodore Dreiser kept writing about Chicago, but he did so while living in New York and setting his novels in the nineteenth century of his youth, his prose becoming gaudier and his themes weaker with each succeeding novel. The promising group of writers who had produced what can be called the birth of Chicago literature, and with it the American city novel, were no longer participating actively in the city's literary development. Nevertheless, almost simultaneously a younger generation emerged to redefine Chicago for their own time and uses.

The writers growing to maturity after 1910, with Sherwood Anderson as the obvious exception, had for the most part been born in the last two decades of the nineteenth century. They had therefore never experienced the America shaped by the agrarian dream and had no personal recollection of Chicago before the Great Fire of 1871. If they had been old enough at the time of the World's Columbian Exposition, they might have visited it with their parents, but had done so without a fully developed critical sense. Where the earlier generation had in its maturity seen the rise and eventual dominance of capitalism as the single viable American Dream, this younger generation of Chicagoans had grown up *with* the dream, taking the very society that had troubled their predecessors for granted, making them in this way—as they themselves believed—the first truly modern generation in American history. Kenny J. Williams has aptly said that "[i]nstead of bemoaning the rawness of the city, the younger writers celebrated the power of Chicago" (1974, 373), and, coupled with a radical desire to liberate themselves from what they conceived to be the antiquated morals of old America, this celebration soon led to the rejuvenation of the city's literary tradition known as the Chicago Renaissance.

Often escaping to the city from a suffocating small-town existence, writers of the 1910s and 1920s found in Chicago sufficient freedom to reject traditional values and experiment with modern attitudes toward sex, marriage, and bohemia. In new journals and magazines such as the *Friday Literary Review* of 1909, *Poetry* of 1912, and the *Little Review*, which printed its first edition in 1914, writers found a ready outlet for their work in which they continued to refine the search for artistic freedom and literary truth that had for many already begun in the small towns of the American Midwest.[87]

Sherwood Anderson

Simultaneously the most typical as well as the most peculiarly atypical representative of the second generation of Chicago writers, Sherwood Anderson was nearing forty when he came to the city in 1913 in order to escape his dull small-town Ohio existence. In 1914, Anderson would come closest to formulating a literary program for

---

87 The *Friday Literary Review*, a supplement to the *Evening Post*, was founded and edited by Irish-born critic Francis Hackett, serving as a radical voice in the city's literary circles and publishing and advocating writers such as George Bernard Shaw and H. G. Wells, as well as local talent corresponding to Hackett's tastes. *Poetry* was the brainchild of Harriet Monroe, who had herself published poetry since the 1880s, most notably "Cantata," read at the dedication of the Auditorium Theatre, and the "Columbian Ode," which served as the official poem of the World's Columbian Exposition. With *Poetry*, the nation's first magazine devoted entirely to verse, she printed the work of such Chicago names as Sherwood Anderson, Carl Sandburg, Edgar Lee Masters and Vachel Lindsay, as well as Robert Frost and Langston Hughes. Her masterstroke, however, was the enlisting of Ezra Pound as "foreign correspondent" from the second issue onward, whose connections resulted in the publication of, in addition to his own poetry, such eminent names as T. S. Eliot, Marianne Moore, Wallace Stevens and William Carlos Williams. Margaret Anderson, the founder of the *Little Review*, was born in 1886 and published in her magazine many of the same names as Monroe's *Poetry*, even enlisting Pound as foreign editor after his fallout with Monroe in 1917. Other important names appearing include Gertude Stein, Djuna Barnes, Hart Crane, William Butler Yeats as well as James Joyce, whose *Ulysses* she introduced to American audiences, an accomplishment earning her a conviction on charges of obscenity.

the Chicago Renaissance when, in the very first issue of the *Little Review*, edited by his good friend Margaret Anderson, he wrote about "The New Note":

> Simply stated, it is a cry for the reinjection of truth and honesty into the craft [...] it is the voice of the new man, come into a new world, proclaiming his right to speak out of the body and soul of youth [...] Whenever he finds himself baffled in drawing a character or in judging one drawn by another, let him thus turn in upon himself, trusting with child-like simplicity and honesty the truth that lives in his own mind (13–15 passim).[88]

Despite this attention to "truth" and the "new," Anderson's first published novel, *Windy McPherson's Son* from 1916, starts out on a surprisingly traditional note; only in its later, and less successful pages, does it turn toward the themes touched upon in the essay. This makes for an interesting novel that, though fundamentally flawed, adds a new perspective to the familiar theme of the Chicago businessman and dramatizes what Anderson saw as his own moral awakening and middle-aged quest for truth. The novel begins in Caxton, Iowa, a small "corn-shipping town" (9), much like Anderson's own Elyria, Ohio, and follows the young boy Sam McPherson as he, endlessly embarrassed by the constant failure of his father to provide for his family, realizes that "the impulse toward bargaining and money get-

---

88   Eric Homberger, in particular, has wondered about the relative lack of a united vision for the Chicago Renaissance, given the contemporary literary events of the Western world. He writes that "one cannot find in the Chicago milieu anything like the programmes, manifestos and obsessive concern for technique which existed in New York and the cosmopolitan centres of Europe" (154). But perhaps Midwestern writers, as Alfred Kazin has suggested, "caught the new sense of scale involved just in moving to a city" to a higher degree than their counterparts in New York, and therefore did little to limit their newfound freedom by obsessing about manifestos, as witnessed by the decidedly expansive nature of much of the work produced during the Chicago Renaissance (1981, 87).

ting [...] [is] the impulse in him most worth cherishing" (41). "In his bed at night he dreamed of dollars" (74), the narration continues, and, having soon exhausted Caxton's possibilities for monetary gain, "the call of the city" (74) comes to him, prompting him at fifteen to leave his successful peanut and popcorn-selling business in the hands of boys still younger and take the train for Chicago, where he has been promised a position in the arms industry. Once in the city, as critic David D. Anderson has pointed out, Sam "subordinates all his human instincts to his goal" (1967, 21) and, following the rough outline of a popular success novel, soon rises to the top of the company, marrying the daughter of the boss in the process. Becoming in this way "the kind of man of whom America boasts before the world" (246), the middle-aged Sam nevertheless eventually realizes, after his wife leaves him and with strong echoes of Upton Sinclair's rhetoric in *The Jungle*, that modern industry is nothing but a "huge meaningless gamble with loaded dice against a credulous public" (250). He consequently decides to leave the "fast greedy living in the city" behind (258), embarking instead on a mysterious quest "wandering about the world seeking Truth" (297).

Improbable as his quest proves to be, the novel clearly parallels Anderson's own break with business and his decision to devote his life to finding truth in literary expression. The point of the novel, and its main interest as part of the Chicago tradition, is the obvious fact that Sam is able to realize the error of his ways without, as was often the case with the first generation of Chicago writers, having it spelled out for him by the striking of an obscure naturalistic force, such as the hotel fire in Robert Herrick's *The Common Lot*. The puzzling quest for Truth turns out to be rather underwhelming for Sam as well as the reader, yet the moment when Sam finds himself writing thoughtlessly on a piece of paper that "the best men spend their lives seeking truth" (240) marks an important shift in Chicago fiction as Anderson, like writers after him, begins to turn inward instead of outward for a solution to problems posed by the city as a symbolic microcosm of American society. By fictionalizing his own break with a lifestyle dictated by business, Anderson's novel becomes a companion piece to his own introspective search for literary truth, a quest that is in turn symbolic of many of the themes touched upon by the Chicago Renaissance.

His next published novel, *Marching Men* from 1917, exhibits many of the same concerns as it explores once again the need for the individual to distill meaning from society, but it differs from *Windy McPherson's Son* by suggesting that in modern American society truth can no longer be located by consciously searching for it. Instead, it must be found at the end of the deliberately chosen road to failure. Beaut McGregor, the protagonist of *Marching Men*, grows up with feelings of intense hatred for the people in his small Pennsylvania town who, "[d]umb with toil" (28), spend their aimless lives digging up coal for a faceless big-city corporation.[89] Beaut's father, a miner himself, dies as he tries to save the lives of colleagues trapped in the shaft, and later his mother's bakery goes bankrupt as she feeds the ungrateful townspeople during a strike. Escaping to Chicago, Beaut soon realizes that the city is only an exaggerated version of small-town Middle America, filled as it is with "a mere disorderly mass of humans cheaply equipped. Everything is cheap. When the people get home to their houses they sit on cheap chairs before cheap tables and eat cheap food. They have given their lives for cheap things" (71). Longing to establish "a powerful brotherhood" (181) among the men estranged from each other by the spiritual emptiness and material cheapness pervading modern American life, Beaut trains as a lawyer before eventually concocting the idea of the Marching Men Movement, in which men will march together, "shoulder to shoulder [...] until the ground shakes and tall buildings tremble" (206).

This plan, of course, comes very close to being a sort of quasi-totalitarian design that is increasingly difficult to ignore as Beaut voices

89   An early draft of *Marching Men* was written while Anderson was still living and working as a businessman in Elyria, Ohio. The manuscript underwent several changes on its way to publication, some of them not authorized by Anderson. The 1972 critical edition edited by Ray Lewis White attempts to recover the author's full intentions, and it has therefore been used here.

his hope that the people of the country "will cease to be individuals. They will become a mass, a moving all-powerful mass" (183) and that "[t]he movement we have started can pay no attention to the whimperers" (185). Unfortunate as his main metaphor would prove to be, it is important to notice that Anderson had in mind not the political unification of America, but instead the reestablishment of intense personal contact between people too long alienated from each other by society. Only through unity can men again become individuals, the book argues, and as its second half unfolds it becomes clear that neither author nor protagonist possess a coherent idea of where the Movement will lead them. In the end, the narrative settles instead for making vague and generalizing statements, such as when Beaut proclaims the Movement to be "the beginning of men's realization of themselves" (185).

In the end, as it becomes evident that the Movement will fail, Anderson nevertheless saves what looks like an impending literary fiasco by returning to the theme begun with Sam McPherson's search for Truth. The final passage, spoken by a rich industrialist, reads: "What if after all this McGregor and his woman knew both roads? What if they, after looking deliberately along the road toward success in life, went without regret along the road to failure? What if McGregor and not myself knew the road to beauty?" (225). While Sam's quest is undeniably motivated by noble sentiments, it nevertheless remains an essentially selfish gesture aimed at securing peace of mind for the individual in a spiritually empty society. In *Marching Men*, conversely, Beaut realizes that the endless striving for bigger and better things inherent in modern American life can only be achieved by negating the definition of one's self within the context of society and by individual reconciliation with the prospect of certain failure, a theme that aligns the novel with the Chicago fiction of Robert Herrick.

These are perplexing novels filled with the muddled logic of a writer not yet fully at ease with his newfound creative powers; but they are interesting because they unashamedly attempt to analyze and define Anderson's own sudden change of life, as well as his desire to understand a society that made this change a matter of such urgent necessity that he left family and business behind, seeking instead to redefine himself as a bohemian in Chicago. Anderson was to publish several more novels, along with volumes of short stories, autobiographical sketches, and free verse poetry. In 1919 he published a collection of interconnected stories entitled *Winesburg, Ohio*, which were his imaginative breakthrough and most lasting contribution to American literature. Because only a few of the stories in *Winesburg, Ohio* employ Chicago as a major setting, his first two novels remain of central importance to the treatment of the city in Anderson's fiction. Both novels convey the liberating power and quest for truth and freedom in literary expression that Anderson himself associated with the city, while bringing a personal perspective and a sense of individual responsibility to many of the themes that the first generation of writers had tried to explain in abstract and naturalistic terms. Where Theodore Dreiser's Carrie Meeber only a decade and a half earlier had been "a waif among forces" existing essentially in a world outside of moral considerations, Anderson's characters define themselves by looking for meaning within themselves and in their relation to society. Sherwood Anderson was in this way the first truly modern writer using Chicago as his source material, and he played an important part in bringing the literary city out of the nineteenth century.

Floyd Dell

If one writer can be said to be symbolic of the Chicago Renaissance, it is Floyd Dell. Born in 1887 to a slightly disreputable family in yet another small Midwestern town, Dell made his way to Davenport, Iowa, working as an apprentice reporter for the local *Times*, and finally to Chicago in 1908, where, the following year, he secured a position as assistant editor for the *Friday Literary Review*. Primarily a critic, Dell helped give early shape to the budding Chicago Renaissance, but he was also among the first to leave the city for New York and Greenwich Village, settling there in 1913 as editor of the radical journal *The Masses*. He continued to involve himself in the Chicago scene, encouraging and publishing writers such as Sherwood Anderson and Carl Sandburg, both of whom he had met during his relatively brief stay in the city. That stay, however, proved to be a pivotal event in his life and turning to fiction in 1920, while still a young man, Dell published the largely autobiographical novel *Moon-Calf*, chronicling the intellectual development of his young hero Felix Fay through several Midwestern towns. The next year, Dell followed Felix to Chicago and its nascent artistic flowering with *The Briary-Bush*.

Moon-Calf can be seen as a prelude to the typical story of the country youth going to Chicago, but given an intellectual spin. Moving from his small hometown of Maple to medium-sized Vickley, where "[a]mbitious boys dreamed of Chicago" (95), thirteen-year-old Felix starts exploring the library and is soon familiar with both literary classics and contemporary radicals—Alexandre Dumas and Robert G. Ingersoll among them—and begins to deliver speeches in school on such topics as "The Influence of Ideas on Civilization" (106). Moving on to the bigger town of Port Royal, built, as it later seems to him, "for growing up in" (394), Felix soon finds himself associating with socialists, anarchists, newspapermen and aristocratic loafers, and after having his heart broken he realizes that in order to succeed as a writer and an intellectual he needs the experience of Chicago. The gradual move from the village to the big city is an important strategy for the novel, allowing Felix to undertake the customary journey step by step, adjusting himself accordingly and setting the stage for his eventual determination that—as he contemplates the lure of Chicago near the beginning of *The Briary-Bush*—he will "go there not as a moonstruck dreamer, but as a realist, able to face the hard facts of life" (4).

Taking an analytical approach to the well-known theme of going from the country to the city, Felix is fully aware of "how unconscious Chicago would remain of the arrival of one more poor struggler" (22). Determined not to let the city get the better of him, he reflects, upon finding the skyscrapers and the "great clouds of white steam" to be almost beautiful, that "doubtless that notion merely proved him to be what he was, a boy from the country" (28). Considering it a mask covering its sinister intentions, Felix dismisses all friendliness encountered in the city as—having apparently read his Dreiser and Norris—calculated "to make an impressionable young man forget that he was a mere unconsidered atom in a cruel chaos" (30), and he is therefore at first distrustful when befriended by a young woman working in the settlement where he goes to live. Her name is Rose-Ann, and she proves to be more knowledgeable about the city than Felix, telling him about the possibilities for the young and the creative: "Chicago wants to be a metropolis. And all the stock-yards in the world won't make a metropolis. Enough of us, given a free-hand—can. And Chicago knows it. Just now we are at a premium here. We can be as crazy as we like!" (34). Chicago, in other words, needs a renaissance, and Felix is soon, and almost without trying, taking an active part in the city's cultural life as a book reviewer for the *Evening Chronicle*. He marries Rose-Ann in a union based on modern ideas of freedom and individuality. There would have been no ceremony at all, Rose-Ann says, had she been "brave enough to dispense with the—rigmarole" (107) but, allowing for this tiny bit of conformity, the rest of the novel sets out to explore their unconventional marriage and what David D. Anderson has called "[t]he spirit of the movement and its confidence that personal freedom and artistic expression are one" (1999, 12). Afraid that a normal apartment will act as a prison in which they will "be like everybody else" (150), and from where "it will take years to break free" (150), the young couple move into a one-room studio on Fifty-seventh Street, an area already populated by artists, and where they soon become the center for parties and all-night conversations over endless cups of coffee.

It eventually becomes clear, though, that their eagerness to embrace the new ideals of freedom in marriage does not translate itself easily to the realities of two people living together as man and wife. As complications culminating in the separation of the two arise, Felix realizes that "[i]t was too easy [...] I came to Chicago expecting to have to fight my way. Chicago was too damned nice too me. I've been living in a pasteboard world ever since" (418). His good fortune of arriving in the city at the dawn of the Chicago Renaissance had failed to provide what he, as a writer, had come to Chicago with intentions of finding, namely, "a world where ideas counted for something—where people might put you in jail if you disagreed with them" (418).

He was instead contented with playing the role, as he consequently calls himself, of "The Intellectual Playboy" (418). In this respect at least, Chicago of the early twentieth century was, in its relatively uncritical eagerness to have a cultural life, not fully the complex metropolis that New York was. But while Dell in real life saw his marriage collapse and went on to Greenwich Village and *The Masses*, his alter ego reunites with his wife and stays in Chicago, discovering that the old dream of freedom was "but a dream only—and worthy only the farewell tribute of a faint and shadowy regret" (425). Perhaps Dell, in retrospect, felt a sense of regret over not having done the same, and the novel ends upon a note that once again combines the personal and the artistic as, in the last pages, Felix plans to build a house for himself and Rose-Ann in which they will live with their discovery that one must be ready to conform a little in order to be truly free.[90]

As was the case with Sherwood Anderson, Chicago and its promise of complete freedom to pursue a literary career had drawn Floyd Dell to its center. But while Anderson came to the city in middle age and operated with the traditional Chicago themes inherited from writers such as Henry B. Fuller and Robert Herrick, Floyd Dell, in the guise of Felix Fay, was a young man in his early twenties when he arrived in the city. Filled with youthful desire, he lacked Anderson's personal maturity and consequently learned the Chicago lesson through heartbreak, leading to the eventual reevaluation of his ideals. Dell ventured further east to New York and a still greater metropolis where, through his involvement with a socialist daily and a lengthy trial for sedition during the First World War, he finally realized the full importance of his Chicago years to his intellectual development.[91]

---

90   Dell's marriage to Margery Currey, whom he had met in much the same way as when Felix meets Rose-Ann, ended in divorce in 1915, after the couple relocated to New York.

91   Upon the U.S. entering the First World War in 1917, Dell and several other writers, editors and cartoonists working for *The Masses* were charged with conspiracy to commit sedition according to the Espionage Act. In the 1918 trial,

The Briary-Bush is the best fictional representation of the Chicago Renaissance and the sense of excitement and liberty that permeated the city's artistic circles during the second decade of the twentieth century. That it was written from the perspective of later years only adds to the fullness of the picture painted, anticipating the short life of an important moment in American thought and literature.

Carl Sandburg

Perhaps the most artistically original and democratically inclusive of the writers associated with the Chicago Renaissance was Carl Sandburg, born in the town of Galesburg, Illinois, to Swedish immigrant parents in 1878. His father was a blacksmith and railroad worker, and Sandburg spent his early working life as a laborer and a bootblack before embarking on a vagabond journey around the Midwest that was eventually to last three years and provide him with an intimate knowledge of the region. Working for two years as secretary to the socialist mayor of Milwaukee, Sandburg arrived in Chicago in 1913 and entered the literary world with a great deal of attention with the publication in *Poetry* the following year of his brazen and expansive "Chicago."[92] In 1916 a collection entitled *Chicago Poems*, named after his first and biggest success, highlighted Sandburg's unique use of the city as subject matter for poetry. The title, of course, was a provocation meant to prove that even a city as rough, and in many ways common, as Chicago could be made to serve the poetic imagination. Where the British nature poets had often been overwhelmed by the exquisite beauty of nature, Sandburg the modern-day romanticist

---

however, the jury failed to agree on a verdict, and a second trial in 1919 went equally undecided. With the war having ended, the charges were dropped, but *The Masses* closed down, causing Dell and his colleagues to start a similar journal entitled *The Liberator* and which ran until 1924.

92 The attention was, almost by default, of both favorable and condemning character. While the poem was hailed as a major event and awarded the Levinson Prize in *Poetry*, it was called "an impudent affront to the poetry-loving public" (quoted by Monroe, 312).

was amazed by the poetic beauty and everyday majesty to be found among the immigrants, cripples, and factory workers of industrial Chicago.

Writing in the free verse style of Whitman, he attempted to give the voluble inclusiveness of the earlier poet a contemporary point of view, documenting the intense variety and excitement of American life and experience. In "Chicago" he famously, as witnessed by parts of the poem having become mottos for the city, begins:

Hog Butcher for the World,
Tool Maker, Stacker of Wheat,
Player with Railroads and the Nation's Freight Handler;
Stormy, husky, brawling,
City of the Big Shoulders (3).[93]

This apparently uncritical and celebratory cataloguing of the city's physical and symbolic greatness, which critic Paul J. Ferlazzo has called "the brawny industrial complex where things are killed, made and moved" (52), is immediately interrupted by Sandburg's surprising admission that "[t]hey tell me that you are wicked and I believe them" (3). Chicago is also the city of "painted women under the gas lamps luring the farm boys" and also of the brutality evident from "the marks of wanton hunger" that the speaker has seen "[o]n the faces of women and children" (3). But as opposed to "the little soft cities," Chicago is "proud to be alive and coarse and strong and cunning" (3), laughing "as an ignorant fighter laughs who has never lost a

---

93   Anyone who has visited Chicago will have noticed especially the first and last lines of the excerpt quoted from Sandburg as being omnipresent in the city's continuing habit of boosterism. The official city motto, Urbs in Horto, Latin for "city in a garden," dates back to the incorporation of Chicago as a city in 1837. The popular motto, however, is "I Will," named after local artist Charles Holloway's drawing of a figure in a decidedly determined stance, and came into being after the *InterOcean* in 1891 sponsored a contest to achieve a design or device comparable to New York's Father Knickerbocker.

battle" and knowing "that under his wrist is the pulse, and under his ribs the heart of the people" (4).

Using the trope of personification, Sandburg paints the picture of an ignorant giant that laughs in the faces of its weaker counterparts, fully aware that it is, as literary critic Charles Molesworth has noted, "the hub of the prairie, the funnel of America's raw materials" (35), and consequently of vital importance to the nation. New York might be the consumer and refiner of American society, but it is Chicago—situated in the middle of the wilderness it has tamed for exploitation—that is the producer and therefore the origin of the country's prosperity. Caring little about tradition in a culture based on the present, Chicago laughs "the stormy, husky, brawling laughter of Youth" (4), knowing in its optimism that it is the worker and not the businessman who is behind the greatness of the country. Needless to say, the role of hog butcher for the world requires a fair amount of white-collar participation, but Sandburg's chief interest in the complex industrial machine remains the common man or woman sweating in the ditches and factories of the pulsating city, some of them falling prey to its often uncaring ambition.[94]

The opening poem introduces the themes that are to be explored throughout the part of the collection directly concerned with Chicago. Had the poems been arranged according to a chronologic series of events describing the life of the typical citizen, the first poem after "Chicago" could well have been "Mamie." She was a young girl who "beat her head against the bars of a little Indiana town," knowing that "there was a big Chicago far off, where all the trains ran" (35). Working now for "six dollars a week in the basement of the Boston store" (35), she is symbolic of the numerous others who have been betrayed by the promise of Chicago, as is the "dago working for a dollar six bits a day" of "The Shovel Man," whose kiss was once "better than all the wild grapes that ever grew in Tuscany" (16), and the eponymous

---

94   For an extended discussion of the influence of socialism upon Sandburg's poetry, see Mark Van Wienen, "Taming the Socialist: Carl Sandburg's Chicago Poems and its Critics" (1991).

"Anna Imroth," who died by "the hand of God and the lack of fire es-
capes" (33), an event that brings the life-cycle of a typical Chicagoan
to its close.

This last poem is a good introduction to Sandburg's consistency, as literary critic Mark Van Wienen has pointed out, "not only in
speaking out on behalf of laborers and the unemployed but also in
blaming the wealthy and the powerful for their predicaments" (91). In
the poem "Onion Days," for example, he mentions first the grueling
work of an Italian immigrant woman picking onions, before shifting
the focus to her wealthy employer who sits in church speculating on
"whether he could word an ad in the *Daily News* so it would bring
more women and girls out to his farm and reduce operating costs"
(28). Chicago might be a giant, Sandburg suggests, but it is majesty
achieved by exploiting an unknowing and predominantly immigrant
population, a population which nevertheless possesses a culture so
vital that not even the grime and abusive nature of the city can defeat
it, as is symbolized by the "rhythmic oompa of the brasses playing a
Polish folk song" in "Picnic Boat" (19). Acknowledging in this way
the individual contribution made by the city's menial workers, and
drawing from them a straight line to the accomplishments of the
city itself as "Freight Handler to the Nation" (4), Sandburg bestows
a kind of downtrodden dignity upon each of the crippled destinies
chronicled in the collection. In the last poem of the series dealing
overtly with Chicago, entitled "Skyscraper," he describes how it is
"the men and women, boys and girls [who] so poured in and out
all day that give[s] the building a soul of dreams and thoughts and
memories" (65). He makes it clear that it is through the people themselves that the city somehow aspires to be more than the sum of its
stone and concrete parts.

Sandburg's poetry can often seem naïve and unsophisticated,
but it was his avowed ambition to write "simple poems for simple
people."[95] In Sandburg's vision of the metropolis, unlike the Chicago

95   See "Carl Sandburg," in *The Norton Anthology of American Literature*,
1885.

of many of the early novelists, it is not the city that makes the people, but instead the people who make the city. By thus making them part of, instead of subject to, what critic William Alexander has called "the grand, tough energies in America" (68), Sandburg created for the first time in Chicago literature the sense that even the men and women occupying the lowest step on the social ladder were part of the glorious procession into the future that had been seen as the city's manifest destiny since its inception.

Willa Cather

In the history of Chicago literature, no writer is perhaps as difficult to place geographically, chronologically and thematically as Willa Cather. Born in Virginia in 1873—three years before Sherwood Anderson—her family joined relatives in rural Nebraska in 1883 before moving to the nearby railroad town Red Cloud the following year. After graduating high school, Cather attended the University of Nebraska in Lincoln for five years, a period in which she worked as a drama critic for the *Nebraska State Journal* and published her first fiction. Cather shortly thereafter moved to Pittsburgh in order to edit the *Home Monthly* and write reviews for the *Leader*, Cather bypassed Chicago entirely on her way to New York, where she settled in 1906 and eventually became the managing editor of *McClure's Magazine*.

While Cather never lived in Chicago, she is nevertheless an important figure in the city's literary history. Continually setting much of her fiction in late-nineteenth-century Nebraska and Colorado, Cather's literary imagination often follows her female characters to Chicago, where they can better fulfill their human and sometimes artistic potential. Published twenty years apart, her two partially Chicago-set novels *The Song of the Lark* from 1915 and *Lucy Gayheart* from 1935 both describe the artistic awakening of a young prairie girl upon her arrival in the big city.[96] The novels are of exceptional

---

96   In 1937, Cather undertook to revise what she considered to be the slightly overwritten style of *The Song of the Lark* and shortened the novel by almost 5 percent in the process. Designed to make the novel correspond more

interest because of the rare female perspective of both author and protagonist, but also because they embody Cather's changing feelings toward both Chicago and the generic small town, a difference that is articulated in terms typical of Chicago literature.

The Song of the Lark is Cather's third novel and is thematically reminiscent of Sherwood Anderson's belief that the freedom to pursue art is only possible in a big city.[97] The novel follows Swedish small-town Colorado girl Thea Kronborg's artistic awakening and eventual success as an opera singer on the New York stage, a journey which also takes her through Chicago—among other places—during her formative years. The novel opens in 1890, with eleven-year-old Thea already considered something of a child prodigy in the small town of Moonstone, Colorado. Her admirers include railroad man Ray Kennedy, who plans to marry her when she is of age, Dr. Howard Archie, who introduces her to literature and intellectual conversation, and finally—and most importantly for her artistic development— her sorrowful German piano teacher, Mr. Wunsch. It is Mr. Wunsch who proclaims that Thea is different from the other "*Americanischen Fräulein*" of the town because she has "*der Geist, die Phantasie*" (99), but he also believes her to be "thornier and sturdier" than the flowers he remembers from Germany: "[N]ot so sweet, but wonderful" (122). A fortunate mix of old and new world qualities, Thea is identified

to her later theory of fiction as she describes it in her famous and programmatic essay "The Novel Démeublé" from 1922, most of the changes are relatively minor and predominantly affect the novel's concluding chapters. Because the Chicago sequences remain largely unaltered, and because the 1937 edition is perhaps a slightly stronger version of the same novel, the revised edition has been used for the present purposes. For a full discussion, see Robin Heyeck and James Woodress, "Willa Cather's Cuts and Revisions in *The Song of the Lark*" (1980).

97   *The Song of the Lark* could be considered Cather's second novel if one accepts her proposition that she wrote *two* first novels, of which the second, *O Pioneers!* from 1913 represented a new beginning in terms of both theme and setting. Cather's *first* "first novel" is the Henry Jamesian *Alexander's Bridge* from 1912, which takes place in Boston.

as "uncommon in a common world" (268), and she spends her early years in Moonstone discovering the sensuous world around her before eventually developing a strong desire to pass beyond its gendered small-town barriers.

The accidental death of Ray Kennedy in a railroad collision leaves Thea with a large sum of money from his life insurance on the condition that she spends the money by taking piano lessons in Chicago. Though her preacher father believes that "big cities were places where people went to lose their identity and to be wicked" (196), Thea nevertheless boards the train as her mother remarks that "[s]he won't come back a little girl" (198). Differing from most similarly themed sequences in Chicago literature, the novel offers no description of the often symbolic train ride from the small town to the big city. Instead Thea is soon provided with comfortable living arrangements and a piano teacher so in tune with his student that he discovers her true talent to be her voice, a realization that propels Thea to take lessons from the famous but conceited Madison Bowers.

It is another realization, however, that is at the center of the novel's Chicago chapters. Unusually incurious about the city, Thea spends most of her time practicing her piano playing, and it is not until her German landlady encourages her that she visits the Art Institute, where she sees the Jules Breton painting that provides the novel's title and gives its heroine her decisive artistic awakening.[98] Feeling

---

98   In a 1901 article about the Chicago Art Institute, Cather mentions the painting and generalizes Thea's appreciation for it: "It is not unlikely that the Chicago Art Institute, with its splendid collection of casts and pictures, has done more for the people of the Middle West than any of the city's great industries. Every farmer boy who goes into the city on a freight train with his father's cattle and every young merchant who goes into the city to order his stock, takes a look at the pictures. There are thousands of people all over the prairies who have seen their first and only good pictures there. They select their favorites and go back to see them year after year. The men grow old and careworn themselves, but they find that these things of beauty are immortally joygiving and immortally young. You will find hundreds of merchants and farmer boys all over Nebraska and Kansas and Iowa who remember Jules Breton's beautiful 'Song of

an "almost boundless satisfaction" when looking at the painting (249), Thea feels her desires and determination intensify, and she soon starts to take full advantage of the cultural opportunities that the city has to offer. In a passage reminiscent of Hamlin Garland's *Rose of Dutcher's Coolly*, Thea attends a concert at the Auditorium Theatre, and the experience proves so overwhelming that her perception of the world, as well of herself, is changed. Emerging out into the dusk after the performance, "[f]or almost the first time Thea was conscious of the city itself, of the congestion of life all about her, of the brutality of power of those streams that flowed in the streets, threatening to drive one under" (253). Much like Theodore Dreiser's Sister Carrie, she is then accosted by two men, the first one exiting a saloon and asking her if she is "[l]ooking for a friend to-night" (253), and the second leaning over to whisper something to her. Unlike Carrie, however, Thea turns the Hurstwoods and the Drouets of the world away, and understands that in order to succeed in the world she must rely on herself and see through the social Darwinist workings of society:

> There was some power abroad in the world bent upon taking away from her that feeling with which she had come out of the concert hall. Everything seemed to sweep down on her to tear it out from under her cape. If one had that, the world became one's enemy; people, buildings, wagons, cars, rushed at one to crush it under, to make one let go of it. Thea glared round her at the crowds, the ugly, sprawling streets, the long lines of lights, and she was not crying now. Her eyes were brighter than even Harsanyi [Thea's piano

the Lark,' and perhaps the ugly little peasant girl standing barefooted among the wheat fields in the early morning has taught some of these people to hear the lark sing for themselves" (1970, 842–843). In a preface to the novel added in 1932, however, Cather calls the painting "rather second-rate" and mentions that the novel's title has often been taken to refer to "the vocal accomplishments of the heroine." This, she continues, "is altogether a mistake. Her song was not of the skylark order" (1937, v).

teacher and friend] had seen them. All these things and people were no longer remote and negligible; they had to be met, they were lined up against her, they were there to take something from her. Very well; they should never have it. They might trample her to death, but they should never have it. As long as she lived that ecstasy was going to be hers. She would live for it, work for it, die for it; but she was going to have it, time after time, height after height. She could hear the crash of the orchestra again, and she rose on the brasses. She would have it, what the trumpets were singing! She would have it, have it – it! Under the old cape she pressed her hands upon her heaving bosom, that was a little girl's no longer (254–255).

Literally growing up right there on the street, the little girl from Moonstone has become a young woman in Chicago. Filled with a new sense of selfhood and purpose, Thea is soon on her way to bigger and better things, a journey taking her first to the Southwest and Mexico, and then to Europe before finally arriving in New York, where the novel ends with Thea as the experienced and successful star of the Metropolitan Opera.

But it is Chicago that is the stage of both her search for independence and her artistic awakening. By revealing its cruel face in the moments after Thea has experienced the intense joy that in Chicago literature is often associated with a musical performance at the Auditorium, the city forces her to focus her attention on herself and her desires in order that she may keep her newfound sense of purpose and direction. But where Dreiser used the naturalistic city to reveal his heroine's moral failings and insisted on her unfulfilled desire at the end of the novel—at a point where Carrie, like Thea, has become a successful artist in New York—Cather's *Künstlerroman* uses the imposing city as a metaphor for a stage in the artist's development that must be faced and transcended if final success is to be achieved. And where Carrie's innocence and small-town background made her susceptible to the temptations of the big city, Moonstone, as critic Susan A. Hallgarth has pointed out, "defines and encourages Thea's talent and inner strength" (171) by serving first as nurturer and then as constrictor of her artistic development. Thea is a hybrid, both of the old world and of the new, but also of small-town values and big-city opportunity—and this combination, Cather implies, produces her eventual success in a city where so many before her have failed. *The Song of the Lark* is often regarded as the most directly autobiographical of Willa Cather's novels, and the story of the development of a young Midwestern girl's artistic faculties certainly shares many similarities with Cather's own life.

If *The Song of the Lark* is in some ways the optimistic counter-part to Dreiser's *Sister Carrie*, then Cather's late novel *Lucy Gayheart* is—within her own oeuvre—the tragic complement to her former novel. Like Thea, Lucy is a young girl from a small town, and while the novel deals with her early years only in summary, Lucy exhibits such a carefree demeanor that it causes her neighbors in Haverford, Nebraska, to conclude years later that "[l]ife seemed to lie very near the surface in her" (5). Unlike Thea, however, who is at all times ut-terly dedicated to her art, Lucy is "talented, but too careless and lighthearted to take herself very seriously" (5) when she first goes to Chicago in 1899, at the age of eighteen. Again omitting the symboli-cal first train ride, Cather instead begins her story in the winter of 1901, when Lucy spends the Christmas vacation of her third year in Chicago with her family in Haverford. Having been courted since childhood by Harry Gordon, the son of the local banker, Lucy is expected by both her family and the townspeople to marry him once she completes her training as a pianist in Chicago. This Christmas, however, Harry becomes aware of a change in her character, and after noting that she is "perhaps a trifle more reserved" (22), he concludes that "Lucy wasn't an artless, happy little country girl any longer; she was headed toward something" (23). In a certain way, Lucy has at the novel's beginning already undergone the transformation experienced by Thea after her visit to the Auditorium, but for her this change has as much to do with the personal freedom promised by Chicago as with its offers of artistic opportunity.

Chicago, for Lucy, is a place "where a window or a doorway or a street corner with a magical meaning might at any moment flash out of the fog" (25). Here, she can "for the first time in her life [...] come and go like a boy" (26), and after spending her vacation at home, she is "glad as never before to be back with her own things and her own will" (27). Where Thea was reluctant and disinterested in the city, Lucy throws herself into it and uses it as a means to liberate herself from her constricting and male-dominated small-town background. Serving in both novels more as symbol than as reality, the Chicago of *Lucy Gayheart* is used throughout the narrative to reflect the young heroine's moods. While the city certainly has "plenty of room to be lonely" and contains many "sad and discouraged people" (62), the Chicago of Lucy's happier days offers views of the lake that are "wrinkled with gold [...] stretching before her unspent and beautiful" (47) and gives one "the freedom to spend one's youth as one pleased, to have one's secret" (86). Strikingly, in a passage echoing both Henry B. Fuller's *The Cliff-Dwellers* and the naturalistic sentiments of writers such as Norris and Dreiser, a despondent Lucy looks at the streets as "narrow rivers, shut in by grey cliffs where the light was always changing, and she herself was a twig or a leaf swept along on the current" (75).

After returning to the city from Haverford, Lucy soon begins a new job accompanying on piano the famous singer Clement Sebastian as he practices in his downtown studio. Lucy quickly develops an infatuation for the older man, and they start a love-affair, with Clement promising to take her with him to New York. During his summer tour of Europe, however, Lucy stays in Chicago, and soon after hears that Sebastian has drowned while swimming in Lake Como. Anguished and disillusioned, Lucy returns to Haverford, but while she still loves the little town, "it was a heartbreaking love, like loving the dead who cannot answer back" (136). Haverford has little to offer her, and Lucy sinks into deep depression for several months before finding within herself the strength to continue with her life and career: "She was young, she was strong, she would show them that they couldn't crush her. She would get away from these people who were cruel and stupid—stupid as the frozen mud in the road. If she let herself think, she would cry. She must not give in to it, she must hurry on" (198). This passage is surprisingly similar—in theme if not in style—to Thea Kronborg's transcendent experience of self-hood in *The Song of the Lark*, but while Cather in the earlier novel let the transformation take place on the streets of Chicago, in *Lucy Gayheart* the small town acts as the metaphoric oppressor that must be overcome by the young and ambitious artist. Chicago, in the later novel, functions as a mirror for Lucy's emotions and state of mind and offers her a chance to see herself freely reflected in its resplendent reality, and to do away with the limiting small-town existence into which she was born.

Almost as soon as she decides to go back to Chicago and fight for her place in life, however, Lucy tragically drowns while skating on the river. The novel's last part tells of Harry Gordon who, twenty-five years after her death, still has fond memories of her. For him, his small-town existence is "a life sentence" (221), and as he studies three light footprints made in wet cement by the young Lucy, he notices that they are "running away" (231). The only tangible impression made by Lucy on the world thus remains in Haverford, and while she perhaps finds in death the freedom she longed for, Cather nevertheless uses the ending to suggest the impossibility of escaping from a small-town background. Where the small town was an important reason for the success of Thea Kronborg in *The Song of the Lark*, in *Lucy Gayheart* it is an obstacle never to be overcome. And while Chicago was the opposition faced by Thea in the earlier novel, it has twenty years later become the stage for Lucy's reinvention of herself.

Having at no point lived in the city, Cather was never associated with the group of writers who constituted the Chicago Renaissance. That her two novels about the city were written twenty years apart and set around the turn of the century makes it difficult to place her in a chronology of Chicago literature. Thematically, too, she moved from the by-then classic view of the city in 1915, which held that it was an obstacle to be overcome by the individual to the belief in 1935 that it offered a young small-town girl both increased freedom and a place in the world. The combination of conventional stories with a fresh and surprisingly rare female perspective, as well as Cather's undeniably powerful and evocative prose, assures the status of her two Chicago-set novels as important to a complete picture of the city's literary history.

Other Voices of the Chicago Renaissance

It is a curious fact of the Chicago Renaissance that many of the best writers usually connected with it only rarely wrote at length about the city itself. Sherwood Anderson, after his first two novels, abandoned the city in favor of the generic small Midwestern town; Floyd Dell wrote little fiction and only after almost a decade in New York did he look back at the Chicago experience; and Carl Sandburg made a name for himself with his *Chicago Poems*, but then turned his eye upon America at large and finally upon Abraham Lincoln, about whom he wrote a six-volume biography that earned him the Pulitzer Prize. Willa Cather never lived in the city and only wrote about it intermittently.

While the movement known as the Chicago Renaissance included several other writers who sometimes wrote about the city, none were more celebrated at the time than Vachel Lindsay, whose "General William Booth Enters into Heaven" caused a minor literary sensation upon its 1913 publication in *Poetry*. A prolific writer of poetry in all styles and genres, Lindsay nevertheless only mentioned Chicago in passing, living most of his life in Springfield and busying himself instead with projects such as basing his poetry on Egyptian hieroglyphics.

With the appearance of *The Spoon River Anthology* in 1915, Edgar Lee Masters, whose first collection of poetry dated back almost twenty years, became something of a national phenomenon. But while he continued to write and publish at a rate of almost one collection a year, he never seemed fully at home in environments other than the small Illinois town of his most popular and sustaining work. One example is a 1916 poem entitled "Chicago," in which he calls the city's skyline "the Sierras of the lakes" (108) and later continues: "From a tower like a mountain promontory / The cesspool of a railroad lies to view, / Fouling the marble of the city's glory" (109). Appearing two years after Sandburg's "Chicago," Masters's poem seems old-fashioned and is lacking almost entirely in both new and memorable images.

Ben Hecht, born in 1893 and among the youngest of the writers associated with the Chicago Renaissance, came to Chicago as a newspaper writer, published intermittently in the *Little Review*, and eventually in 1922 saw his columns for the *Daily News* collected in a rather unremarkable volume entitled *A Thousand and One Afternoons in Chicago*. Of more interest is the novel *Erik Dorn*, published the previous year, which is a chronicle of the intense spiritual emptiness and lack of purpose experienced by the title character in Chicago of the early 1920s: "A tawdry pantomime was life, a pouring of blood, a grappling with shadows, a digging of graves. 'Empty, empty,' his intelligence whispered in its depths, 'a make-believe of lusts. What else? Nothing, nothing. Laws, ambitions, conventions—froth in an empty glass'" (18). The novel eventually overflows with such exuberantly youthful gloom, and Dorn presently rebels against the constraints of society and a loveless marriage, leaving for Europe and a series of invigorating adventures.

By the early 1920s, at about the same time that Floyd Dell was remembering in New York his youthful experiences in Chicago, the Renaissance had already largely run its course, and the mild attempts at rebellion against the standards of old-fashioned society seemed quaint to the new generation growing into maturity in the Jazz Age of the 1920s. Writers such as F. Scott Fitzgerald and Ernest Hemingway—both Midwesterners and the latter an actual Chicagoan—would later admit to having learned much about writing from the economic and suggestive prose of Sherwood Anderson. But Fitzgerald later declared that "*The Briary Bush* [sic] is stinko" and, even earlier, chose to leave out Chicago entirely in his journey from St. Paul and Minnesota to the American East and across the Atlantic to Paris and the European centers of modernism.[99]

The movement east was a typical one, even for writers who had

---

99   Fitzgerald's short remark is inserted rather randomly into a letter, dated January 24, 1922, to his friend Edmund Wilson, which is reprinted in the

once been closely affiliated with the Chicago scene. In 1916 Margaret Anderson moved the *Little Review* to New York, taking with her, as David D. Anderson notes, "much of the fire of liberation" (1978, 68). She would soon leave New York behind for Paris, as so many other young writers and intellectuals of the late 1910s and early 1920s were to do. Sherwood Anderson, in his *Memoirs*, looked back at his years in Chicago and concluded the movement to be "a Robin's Egg Renaissance [...] It fell out of the nest" (317), and by the mid-1920s the Chicago Renaissance was a thing of the past, prompting literary editor of the *Daily News* Harry Hansen to publish a volume of memoirs as *Midwest Portraits* in 1923, a book that functions as an epitaph for the movement.

In a 1920 article for the *Nation* of London, H. L. Mencken had written about the city that it had given its writers "an impulse toward independence, toward honesty, toward a peculiar vividness and *naivete*—in brief, toward the unaffected self-expression that is at the bottom of sound art" (quoted in Williams 1974, 372). But only a few years later, Chicago evidently had little left to offer by way of freedom and inspiration desired by an increasingly urbane population of artistically minded young men and women, and the city became instead predominantly associated with the gangsters and crime related to prohibition. However, the importance of the Chicago Renaissance as a forerunner to American modernism is captured in cultural historian Hugh Dalziel Duncan's assertion that "[t]he famous revolt of the younger generation which flamed to greatness in the work of Hemingway and T. S. Eliot originated in Chicago where writers were determined to bring literature back to life" (1964, 145). It nevertheless remains a peculiarity of American literary history that Chicago, perhaps the most modern of all American cities, should in the end prove to be uncongenial to the literary movement of modernism.

collection of Fitzgerald's essays, letters and notebooks edited by Wilson and published in 1945 as *The Crack-Up* (1956), 257.

—4—
Inheriting the City, 1923–1953

The Great Depression and the
Neighborhood Novel

After the almost complete literary exodus of the late 1910s and early 1920s, as Chicago was left behind by virtually all of its major writers, the city sank into an intellectual slump and became known as the national capital of organized crime, a development, however, that did little to halt the extraordinary growth of the city. The population reached the three-million mark by the 1920s, a decade of unprecedented material prosperity in American history that was fueled by the wild speculation and inflated stock prices that were eventually to culminate in the economic and social catastrophe of the Great Depression.

With the stock market crash of October 29, 1929, Chicago's hopes for the future were replaced with despair as it became clear that almost a century of unparalleled progress had come to an end. The city's stagnation is symbolized in its census figures: While the population had skyrocketed with almost 700,000 new inhabitants during the 1920s, it added only slightly more than an additional 20,000 by the end of the following decade. Discussing the city's apparent case of arrested development, and bearing testimony to the influence of the rhetoric of Carl Sandburg, journalist A. J. Liebling wrote in 1952 that in the early decades of the century "the city did approximate the great, howling, hurrying, hog-butchering, hog-mannered challenger for the empire of the world specified in the legend, but that at some time around 1930 it stopped as suddenly as a front-running horse at the head of the stretch with a poor man's last two dollars on its nose" (12). Mirroring the closure of the American frontier proclaimed by Frederick Jackson Turner in 1893, the Great Depression forced a city that had hitherto defined itself by its ambition to be first in the world to redefine its purpose and look inward instead of outward.

In literature, as well, the history of Chicago had been largely defined by its attempts to find symbolic meaning in the clamoring spectacle of the modern city. Writers had crafted metaphors and literary strategies in the hope of coming nearer an understanding of Chicago in its entirety, an approach that Floyd Dell, with almost prophetic clarity, had commented on as early as 1913 in an article in the *Bookman*:

> Chicago writers have been obsessed with Chicago. It has appealed to them as a problem rather than as a vast and splendid collection of fictional materials. And so they have not written about any place in particular, they have written about Chicago in general. During the next generation we may expect the novels laid in Chicago to take Chicago more for granted, and to settle down to the business of conveying whatever aspects of its life has excited the novelist to the writing-point. When there cease to be novels "about" Chicago, then Chicago will really have its novels (275).

With the 1930s and the appearance on the Chicago literary map of such figures as James T. Farrell and Richard Wright, the city no longer suggested the image of a unified organism driven by the forces of industrial capitalism. Instead, as Kenny J. Williams has indicated, "[w]riters turned their attention to their urban neighborhoods which somehow were used to symbolize the meaning of the city just as the city had for Fuller and Herrick symbolized America" (374). By finding a microcosm within the microcosm, and by linking their writing to the Sociology Department at the University of Chicago—the nation's foremost investigator of urban conditions and gang-culture—the new generation of writers sought to focus on the immediate environment of their protagonists, whose doings were often con-

tained within the space of a few city blocks.[100] This inspired a literature of the neighborhood, dedicated, as literary critic Carlo Rotella
has written, to "rendering as literature the language, habits and daily
routines of people largely excluded or exoticized by the genteel tradition" (49). In the hope of achieving through a focus on minutiae a
sense of the desperation felt by so many of these people, whether second generation Irish immigrants or first generation black migrants, it
became a literature of the outsider in Chicago and, on a larger scale,
in American society as a whole.

James T. Farrell

As both a chronicle of the changing fortunes of a middle class
Chicago neighborhood from the late 1910s to the early 1930s, as well
as an intensely personal narrative following one character from ado-
lescence to premature death at the age of 29, James T. Farrell's *Studs
Lonigan* trilogy is, in scale and humanity, an impressive literary statement. Born in 1904, Farrell grew up in the Irish part of Chicago's
South Side neighborhood that was to feature prominently in almost
all of his realistic fiction. This neighborhood, he wrote in an essay
entitled "How *Studs Lonigan* Was Written," was "several steps removed from the slums and dire economic want" (1945, 86–87). Never
excelling in anything except baseball while in school, Farrell started
writing fiction only after intermittently attending the University of
Chicago—taking, among other subjects, classes in sociology—and
began there a short story that was eventually to expand into his trilogy of novels chronicling the life and death of Studs Lonigan.[101]

---

100   For a recent and excellent book-length treatment of the influence of
the Chicago School of Sociology upon the novels of especially Farrell, Wright
and Nelson Algren, see Carla Cappetti, *Writing Chicago: Modernism, Ethnography, and the Novel* (1993).

101   The first volume of the trilogy, *Young Lonigan*, was published in 1932,
the middle volume, *The Young Manhood of Studs Lonigan*, in 1934, and *Judgment
Day*, the final and concluding volume, in 1935. The three novels were collected
as one volume for the first time in 1935 and have seen little separate publishing

The Chicago of *Studs Lonigan* is, for the most part, limited to the blocks around the intersection of Fifty-eighth Street and Prairie Avenue. The specifics of the neighborhood include such landmarks as "Frank Hertzog's shoe repair shop, about fifty yards or so down from the corner" (164), "Schreiber's ice cream parlor," standing "between Prairie and Indiana on Fifty-eighth" (124), and the place where Studs and the gang spend the largest part of their idle days, "Bathcellar's Billiard Parlor and Barber Shop," situated "two doors east of the elevated station" on Fifty-eighth Street, "midway between Calumet and Prairie Avenues" (118).[102] In many ways reminiscent of a small town, the area is predominantly inhabited by second-generation Irish immigrants who have moved to a place in society beyond immediate want, with many of them owning buildings and small companies in the area. Studs's father, a prosperous painting contractor, is a good example, owning the building in which the family lives and proudly offering his oldest son "a good home, a good example set for him, a place made for him in life, all that a young man could ask for" (297). As the book opens in 1916, fourteen-year-old Studs, whose real name is William, is graduating from St. Patrick's grammar school and must choose the direction of his future life. While his pious mother is urging him to join the priesthood—and privately admits that "I make novenas that God will give him the call" (45)—Studs's father is looking forward to having his son help out with the business, believing that "a father had some right to expect something in return when he did so much for his children" (45). Studs, however, heeds the call

since then. As the trilogy is generally regarded as one novel, and as it makes little or no sense for the present purposes to treat *Studs Lonigan* as three separate works, the volumes will in the following be considered and referred to as one.

102   The part of Fifty-eighth Street where *Studs Lonigan* takes place is not immediately close to the Fifty-seventh Street where Floyd Dell's Felix Fay tried his hand at intellectual bohemia. Separated by the immense Washington Park, the western part of the street was (and still is) a neighborhood entirely different from the eastern part, which cuts through the University of Chicago campus in the middle of the wealthy Hyde Park area.

for neither religion nor business and drifts instead into the Fifty-eighth Street gang, where he becomes involved in delinquencies such as raiding candy stores and fighting the other gangs of the neighborhood, especially those consisting mostly of Jews and blacks, who are lowest in the area's racial hierarchy.

His hopes and dreams inspired by the American democratic ideal, Studs, as literary critic Daniel Shiffman has noticed, "identifies himself with war heroes and sport stars; he can't consider a life for himself that is in any way ordinary" (70). When his commonplace existence, relatively comfortable as it is, fails to live up to the promise made by the movies, newspapers and popular history, he defines himself in the context of the gang and, within that, by his ability to be "tough," suppressing his emotions and desires to the point of non-existence. His childhood romance with a neighborhood girl named Lucy, for example, comes to an end when a boy from the gang sees the couple in the park, embarrassing Studs and causing him to reflect that "loving a girl the way he loved Lucy was goofy, because a big tough guy should only want to jump a girl, and think that all the rest and the love was crap" (178). Losing his virginity in a "gang-shag" with an adventurous local girl (148), he secretly idolizes the purity and slightly higher social class of Lucy and consequently measures his life largely in terms of how well it compares to a life spent with her. Unable to find satisfaction or a sense of aim and purpose on the streets, Studs nearly destroys himself with prohibition-era bootleg whiskey before finally—after a case of particularly self-destructive behavior followed by a narrow escape from "Johnny Law" (311)—deciding to clean up his act and settle down, working for his father as a house painter.

Once he is off the streets, however, Studs is subjected to another set of corrupt and ill-advised values, this time coming from both his family and the Catholic Church. His complacent father cares for little else than his business, his mother is a religious fanatic, and in church Father Shannon frequently sermonizes against "such movements as jazz, atheism, free-love, companionate marriage, birth-control" (414) and condemns "those seats of the godless—the universities—those iniquitous incubators of vice, cheapness and trash—the movies" (415), as well as a variety of literary figures, ranging from the "misguided" (414) Percy Bysshe Shelley to such "windbags and publicity seekers" as H. G. Wells and Sinclair Lewis (418). While Studs and his friends are heavily prejudiced against Jews and blacks and go "searching for niggers" (214) during the 1919 race riots, it is evident that the younger generation have inherited many of these sentiments, exemplified by Studs's father blaming the "shines" for ruining the neighborhood simply by moving into it, as well as his mother's conviction that "niggers haven't got a soul" (433).[103] Racial prejudice, in any form, is an accepted attitude within the community, and Jews and blacks are used as scapegoats for the evils of society, such as when Old Lonigan blames "the Jew international bankers" for the troubles caused by the Depression (783).

The narrow-minded and intolerant environment offers little to nurture personal growth, and as literary critic Robert Butler has argued, "it becomes a trap for Studs Lonigan, whose limited consciousness never allows him to grasp the options available to him" (110). He sinks instead back into the streets and the gangs, looking there for what critic Carla Cappetti has called "an outlet for the impulses that his cultural environment denies" (113). This time, however, his health is ruined for good when on New Year's Eve, 1929, his bubble of excess symbolically bursts, and he is left "bloody, dirty, odorous with vomit" on the curb (459). That he survives is a miracle, his mother believes, but when he is finally well enough to begin life again, the Depression has taken its toll on his already limited options. He finally contracts pneumonia while searching for work and dies the death of a man who has realized that he is indeed nothing but "an all-around no-soap guy" (649).

James T. Farrell, as literary critic Donald Pizer has observed, "was deeply moved by the American dilemma of the warping of potential-

---

103   In an interesting irony, the Lonigans and their neighbors fail to understand that when real-estate prices go down as a result of several blacks moving into the area, it is not the fault of the "greasy, dirty niggers" but of their own bigotry and intolerance (433).

ly admirable yet weak minds by the overwhelming attraction of socially corrupt goals and values" (1982, 72). *Studs Lonigan* demonstrates,
slowly and confidently, how its protagonist's blind and unfaltering
faith in both the American Dream, and the belief that he—Studs
Lonigan!—was born for bigger things, leads in the end only to disil-
lusion and an increased sense of loneliness. And while Chicago is
never as much of an active character as it is in the novels of Theodore
Dreiser and Upton Sinclair, the environment of the neighborhood
microcosm—which manifests, Farrell has noted, "a pervasive spiritual poverty" (1945, 87)—permeates every page and every decision
made, its drab realities and symbolic significance restricting in true
naturalistic fashion the interconnected fate and mental life of its inhabitants.

Richard Wright

Between 1910 and 1940, during the years of the "Great Migration,"
Chicago's black population increased from 44,000 to 278,000, rep-
resenting a phenomenal increase of 530 percent—a rate almost ten
times that of the city's overall population growth in the same three
decades.[104] Escaping from a racist and segregated South, blacks came
to the city looking for jobs as well as relative freedom from prejudice
and a chance to assert themselves as individuals, unfettered by the
color of their skin.

Richard Wright, who had been born in Mississippi in 1908 and
lived with various relatives in different parts of the South, made
his way to Chicago in 1927. Remembering his arrival in the city in
the second volume of his autobiography, entitled *American Hunger*,
Wright poetically stresses his alienation and disappointment upon
first sight of his future home: "Chicago depressed and dismayed me,
mocked all my fantasies. Chicago seemed an unreal city whose mythical houses were built of slabs of black coal wreathed in palls of gray

---

104   Black population numbers according to Graham, 280. The city's population, according to the U.S. Census, grew from almost 2.2 million to 3.4 million during this period, signifying a 55 percent increase.

smoke, houses whose foundations were sinking slowly into the dank prairie" (1).[105] Making his way around the city, it soon dawned on him that while it was relatively free from the overt racial discrimination of his native South, another kind of institutional racism was working behind the scenes and caused him to discern that "this machine-city was governed by strange laws and I wondered if I could ever learn them" (2).

Observing that blacks have historically merely inhabited cities without having an actual claim to them, novelist Toni Morrison has argued that "they could not share what even the poorest white factory worker or white welfare recipient could feel: that in some way the city belonged to them" (1981, 37). Wright felt this predicament in Chicago, confined to the black South Side ghetto and noticing that "[w]herever my eyes turned they saw stricken, frightened black faces trying vainly to cope with a civilization that they did not understand" (3). Being treated with relative indifference—Wright mentions that "[e]ach person seemed to regard the other as a part of the city landscape" (2)—was certainly better than the open hostility toward blacks in the South, but, on the other hand, it was exactly this indifference

---

105   Wright's two autobiographical volumes, entitled *Black Boy: A Record of Childhood and Youth* and *American Hunger*, were originally composed as a single manuscript in 1943, bearing the title of the latter volume. At the urging of his publisher, who believed the second part chronicling Wright's experiences as a member of the Communist Party to be irreconcilable with the book being offered as a selection of the Book-of-the-Month Club, Wright agreed to publish the first part as a separate text called *Black Boy* in 1945. The second part saw scattered publication during Wright's lifetime, most notably as two incomplete installments in the *Atlantic Monthly* under the title "I tried to be a Communist" in 1944, and it was not until 1977, seventeen years after his death, that the complete text was issued as *American Hunger*. The 1991 Library of America edition incorporates the two volumes into one and returns the text to the original transition between the two segments, a passage that had been changed slightly to accommodate the original publication of *Black Boy*. As it provides the full statement of Wright's experiences in Chicago, the original 1977 edition of *American Hunger* has been used for the present purposes.

and pretense of racial equality that was governing the black people of Chicago. Being constantly told that in the northern city racial boundaries were virtually non-existent, and that all men were equal and therefore responsible for their own lives, blacks were made to believe that they were in a position of some power—and therefore had only themselves to blame for their misfortunes. In reality, the white majority was carefully regulating the lives of the city's black population through their total economic, political, and social power.

In his two first novels, *Lawd Today* and *Native Son*, Wright explores with impressive clarity the consequences of the black individual having been numbed into submission by a combination of the white metropolis and what writer Amiri Baraka has called the "environmental social madness" of the South Side black belt (150).[106] The area of the two novels is roughly the same as described in *Studs Lonigan*, only now, ten or fifteen years later, the exodus of the Irish upon the arrival of the blacks is complete, and the rapidly decaying neighborhood has consequently become an almost exclusively black ghetto.[107] Continuing the comparison, *Lawd Today* recycles many of

---

106   *Lawd Today*, Wright's first novel, was begun in 1930 and worked on until at least 1938. Considered to be too controversial in its unflattering description of the spiritual wasteland of the South Side ghetto, the manuscript, originally entitled *Cesspool*, was rejected by every publisher approached by Wright, and it was consequently not until 1963, three years after his death, that the novel finally saw publication. Greeted at the time with a mixture of confusion and hostility, the novel has since been the subject of extensive critical reevaluation and remains an important statement of what Wright considered to be "the essential bleakness of black life" (quoted in Leary, 412). For an overview of the novel's critical reception, as well as an exploration of Wright's political agenda with the novel, see Brannon Costello, "Richard Wright's *Lawd Today!* and the Political Uses of Modernism" (2003). The exclamation point in Costello's title stems from the 1991 Library of America edition, which incorporates several changes into the text, none of which, however, are of substantial character.

107   The neighborhood having become a ghetto, it is plausible to assume that the Lonigans were right when fearing the black invasion in the following terms: "Did you ever look out of the window of the elevated train when you go

the same themes that preoccupied Farrell, and the novel functions as a condensed version of his trilogy, as seen some years later from a black perspective in the same neighborhood, and also ending with the death of its main character. Where *Studs Lonigan* spanned some eight hundred pages and fifteen years in the life of its spiritually numbed protagonist, Wright's novel is short and takes place during a single day. That day, it is evident from the frequent interpolation of snippets of radio broadcasts into the narrative, is February twelfth, the birthday of Abraham Lincoln, known as the Great Emancipator and also, as critic Brannon Costello points out, "icon of bootstraps ideology" (47). The irony of both connotations becomes evident in the course of the day, which opens with an image of a black man futilely climbing a seemingly endless set of stairs, but determined to reach the top by his own effort. Relieved to find the Sisyphean stair-case only a dream, Jake, the main character, eventually wakes up to the smell of bacon and fresh coffee, circumstances that nevertheless do not prevent him from being in a foul mood and verbally abusing and beating his helpless wife Lil.

Jake, as it turns out, is a truly despicable creature, inhabiting a slum world of pool rooms and run-down movie-houses, street magicians and con artists, and where it is considered an accomplishment not to be in jail. Working in the post office as a mail sorter, he is, as critic Yoshinobu Hakutani has observed, "unaware that industrialization and capitalism have hopelessly corrupted his soul" (57). So warped are his values that he subscribes uncritically to the same ideology as the system that is essentially exploiting him: "Nobody but lazy folks can starve in this country" (33) he tells Lil after having declared, without implicit criticism, that "[c]old, hard cash runs this country, always did and always will" (28). Proceeding to dismiss the Democrats as "crazy troublemakers! They ain't got no money," he defiantly asks her

downtown and see what kind of places they live in? God Almighty, such dirt and filth" (433); but since it is of course impossible to blame the blacks for living only in what their economic and social position makes possible, Farrell's irony is nevertheless clear.

"who's going to tell old man Morgan and old man Rockefeller and old man Ford what to do? Who? WHO? [...] Why them men owns and runs the country!" (29). A modern-day slave, Jake has also internalized the racial prejudice of his white masters as his own, and repeats a tirade familiar to working-class whites during the years of the Great Depression, one that Old Lonigan would probably agree with: "That's what's wrong with this country, too many Jews, Dagos, Hunkies, and Mexicans [...] they got the country sewed up; every store you see is run by a Jew, and the foreigners. And they don't think about nobody but themselves. They ought to send 'em all back where they came from" (31).[108]

Having no intellectual powers to see beyond such damaging rhetoric, Jake uncritically believes, like Studs, in what Costello has called "the exploitive myths of American popular culture" (46), a belief that keeps him in the "Squirrel Cage" (99) of the Chicago South Side slum mentioned by Wright in the title of the novel's second part. Like Farrell, Wright had connections to the University of Chicago's Department of Sociology, and indeed the novel reads like the case study of a lost young man oppressed by his environment, the veiled racism of society, and the myth of the American Dream. The result is complete destruction of his individuality, and never once does he cross the boundary from unthinking acceptance to partial illumination of the causes for his desperate situation, but dies in the end from cuts inflicted by his wife in self-defense. Only with the publication of the next novel, *Native Son*, from 1940, was Wright ready to let his main character cross that boundary, showing the gradual develop-

---

108 Lonigan, frustrated by the failing of his business, tells his son: "Well, Bill, tell you, you know for years all these foreigners have been let into America, and now they've just about damn near taken this country over. Why, from the looks of things, pretty soon a white man won't feel at home here. What with the Jew international bankers holding all the money here, and the Polacks and Bohunks squeezing the Irish out of politics, it's getting to be no place for a white man to live" (697).

ment of analytical powers and a heightened sense of self in a young black man.[109]

Bigger Thomas, the hero of *Native Son*, begins as a character slightly more aware of the racist mechanisms of the city than *Lawd Today*'s Jake, but he only remains capable of articulating his situation in very simple terms: "We black and they white. They got things and we ain't. They do things and we can't. It's just like being in jail. Half the time I feel like I'm on the outside of the world peeping in through a knot-hole in the fence" (23). Bigger's entrapment is further illustrated by the airplanes circling over the city, symbolizing the freedom of movement he has never felt and causing him to state ambitiously that "I *could* fly a plane if I had a chance" (20), to which his friend Gus dryly replies, "If you wasn't black and if you had some money and if they'd let you go to that aviation school, you *could* fly a plane" (21). Bigger has, unlike Jake, been programmed into submission not by an empty belief in equal opportunities but by being constantly reminded of the limited possibilities in his essentially meaningless existence. Wright, in an essay entitled "How 'Bigger' Was Born," generalizes Bigger and calls him a "meaningful and prophetic symbol" (xiv), before explaining about the novel's setting:

> The urban environment of Chicago, affording a more stimulating life, made the negro Bigger Thomases react more violently than even in the South [...] It was not that Chicago segregated Negroes more than the South, but that Chicago had more to offer, that Chicago's physical aspect—noisy, crowded, filled with a sense of power and fulfillment—did so much more to dazzle the mind with a taunting sense of possible achievement that the segregation it did

109 Wright had moved to New York in 1937, but retained Chicago as the setting for the novel. The city of his first encounter with urban culture, Chicago was at the time a comparatively new destination for blacks, and consequently both considerably less integrated and without the established black community of New York's Harlem.

impose brought forth from Bigger a reaction more obstreperous than in the South (xv).

That reaction is the brutal killing of Mary Dalton, daughter of the NAACP-supporting millionaire for whom Bigger is sent by the social services to work as a driver. In a misguided attempt to befriend Bigger, Mary and her Communist boyfriend Jan insist that he drive them to "one of those places where colored people eat" (69). But so fearful is he of the power of whites to control and limit his life that he proves entirely unable to relate to white people when given the chance, stammering only a "yessuh" or a "yessum" when addressed.[110] As literary critic Maryemma Graham has noted, Wright wanted to bring Bigger "into a series of complex relationships that his consciousness was not sufficiently developed to handle" (287) and after a night of terror and confusion he is mentally exhausted to the point that his behavior is conditioned almost exclusively by his uncontrollable fear of whites. Upon bringing the drunk Mary home and helping her into bed, Bigger is surprised in her room by the blind mother, and fearing that she will notice his presence and misinterpret his intentions as attempted rape he accidentally smothers Mary with a pillow while trying to keep her silent. Concealing the murder by burning the body in the furnace and blaming the disappearance on Jan, who is, after all, a Communist and therefore, according to the logic of the times, a prime suspect, Bigger stays calm and proceeds to act normally within the white household. The truth is eventually discovered, and Bigger flees back into the Black Belt before he is finally caught, brought to trial, and sentenced to death.

The murder is the defining moment for both Bigger and the

110　While Mary's intentions in trying to make friends with Bigger are without a doubt sincere, she nevertheless betrays her failure to see him as an individual by mentioning, before leaving the house to meet Jan, that she is "going to meet a friend of mine who is also a friend of yours" referring to his Communist allegiances and thereby reducing Bigger once again to his race, without considering his individuality (65).

novel. Where he had been merely a passive presence in the world, he is now, for the first time in his young life, an actor and individual discovering the feeling of power associated with the manipulation of his surroundings: "*He* had done this. *He* had brought all this about. In all of his life these two murders were the most meaningful things that had ever happened to him. He was living, truly and deeply [...] Never had he had the chance to live out the consequences of his actions; never had his will been so free as in this night and day of fear and murder and flight" (225). Transcending his environment, Bigger is doing what nobody thought him capable of doing. Indeed, Yoshinobu Hakutani has pointed out that "the problem of race, the avowed conflict between Black and White people, becomes the catalyst for Bigger's manhood" (59). This conflict is defined in large part in terms of physical position within the city. When Bigger goes to work for the Daltons he is not simply leaving his neighborhood for another, he is entering into a world distinctly different from his own, and where he does not have the necessary social skills to function on an equal footing with the whites that surround him. Moreover, Wright inserts an irony reminiscent of classical tragedy when Bigger discovers that it is the benevolent Mr. Dalton himself who owns the rat-infested building he inhabits with his family: "He owned property all over the Black Belt, and he owned property where white folks lived too. But Bigger could not live in a building across the 'line.' Even though Mr. Dalton gave millions of dollars for Negro education, he would rent houses to Negroes only in this prescribed area, this corner of the city crumbling down from rot" (164). In this unambiguous way, Wright suggests, Mr. Dalton has contributed to the very oppression of the city's blacks that has rendered Bigger Thomas unable to respond with little else than fear and violence when approached by a white man, and he is in the final analysis, therefore, an indirect participant in the death of his own daughter.

This kind of sociological determinism is concomitant with Wright's interest in the findings of the Chicago School of Sociology, which viewed, critic Lawrence R. Rodgers has argued, "the black adjustment to northern cities not as a failure of the individual conditioning or genetic deficiencies, but as an ill-fated, yet rational group response to a combination of environmental pressure and deficit culture" (9). Providing Wright with a sophisticated theory for the expression of his ideas, the last part of the novel is given over almost entirely to a sociological discourse regarding the influence of the environment on the individual. In both *Lawd Today* and *Native Son*, two novels whose immense qualitative difference is determined as much by their subject matter as by the literary skills of their author at the time of writing, Wright explores the effect of a spiritually numbing environment on two characters, one of whom is beyond redemption and never experiences a moment of crucial insight, and the other who only through murder and extortion can begin to slowly understand himself and his capabilities as a human being in Chicago.

Nelson Algren

Among Chicago's neighborhood writers of the 1930s and 1940s, Nelson Algren stands out because of his unflinching insistence upon the essential humanity of his criminal and often depraved characters. Algren became known early in his career as the "poet of the Chicago slums" (Cowley, 614), and famous author and broadcaster Studs Terkel has admiringly said about him that he "goes behind the billboards" and speaks "for those who have no defense" (Algren 1986, 288, 289). Of mixed Scandinavian and Jewish descent, Algren was born in Detroit in 1909, but a few years later he moved with his family first to Chicago's South Side and later to the predominantly Polish Northwest Side. It was this neighborhood that provided him with material for numerous short stories, collected as *The Neon Wilderness* in 1947, as well as the novels *Never Come Morning* and *The Man with the Golden Arm*, which chronicle the lives of hustlers, junkies and prostitutes in the area.

Algren never tired of quoting Whitman's declaration that "I feel I am of them— / I belong to those convicts and prostitutes myself— / And henceforth I will not deny them— / For how can I deny myself?" He identified closely with the outcasts of American society and was on a veritable literary mission to show the general public, as one of his characters phrases it, that "we are all members of one another" (1950, 198).[111] What critic Brooke Horvath has called his "emotional investment in discarded souls" (79) became his acknowledged literary credo, and by bringing the underbelly of Chicago to vibrant life, he attempted to reveal the moral failings of respectable society. In order to preserve their values and perspectives, Algren believed, the middle classes needed and indirectly maintained an element of vice, and consequently reduced what early-century reformers such as Jacob A. Riis had called "the other half" to a stereotype.[112] Through a combination of a classical naturalistic style with a poet's attention to language and concern for symbols, Algren granted his subjects the humanity and individuality which public opinion denied them. Only in "the marginal elements of society," as critic James A. Lewin has pointed out with respect to Algren's approach, can "we see the clearest representation of who we, as the literate and cultured elite, really are" (113).

After the somewhat unsuccessful publication of several short stories and, in 1935, his first novel *Somebody in Boots*, which takes place among disenfranchised drifters in the Depression-era South, Algren joined the Federal Writers' Project in 1936.[113] Here he developed the

---

111   The lines from Whitman's *Leaves of Grass* serve as the epigraph to *Never Come Morning*, from which they are here quoted, and Algren expanded upon the meaning in his preface to the 1963 edition.

112   Jacob A. Riis was a social reformer, muckraking journalist and photographer in turn-of-the-century New York City. He is best known for his pioneering 1890 book of photojournalism entitled *How the Other Half Lives: Studies Among the Tenements of New York*, which brought the city's slums to national attention and caused then-Police Commissioner Theodore Roosevelt to close down the poor-houses run by the city's police department. Riis's book is also commonly cited as an inspiration for Jack London's *People of the Abyss* (1903), his exposé of London's Whitechapel area.

113   The Federal Writers' Project, a part of the Works Projects Administration, was an ambitious New Deal program during the Depression. It employed writers in order to produce local and state guidebooks containing essays on everything from culture to commerce, as well as documenting the folk backgrounds of the region in question. Working for the FWP, Algren met and as-

journalistic skill of documentation and combined it with what folk-lorist B. A. Botkin has called the Project's "synthesis of anthropology, sociology, psychology, and literature" (11). Newly equipped with a diverse set of skills and theoretical frameworks, Algren started work on his second novel, which was published in 1942 as *Never Come Morning.*[114]

In Depression-era Chicago literature, few characters are as determined by their environment as Bruno Bicek, the protagonist of *Never Come Morning.* Bruno, known to his fellow *Chicagoski* in his Northwest Side neighborhood as Bruno Biceps because of his boxing abilities, is seventeen years old when the novel opens and has only rarely been outside of "the Triangle formed by Chicago, Ashland and Milwaukee Avenues" (8). An extreme example of the circumscribed South Side neighborhoods of Farrell and Wright, the Triangle spans only a few city blocks and causes Bruno to reflect, after he and his gang get away with a slot machine after a violent robbery in another part of town, that "he had been out of the Triangle and into the world" (25). Life in the Triangle is lived "beneath the shadow of the El," under which Bruno experiences sunlight "as others recall it seen first through trees or climbing vines" (29). Despite this metaphor, Algren's Chicago is not a Sinclairian jungle of active and dangerous forces acting upon his life, but instead a vast, indifferent "city wilder-

---

sociated with such future Chicago authors as Saul Bellow, Studs Terkel, Gwendolyn Brooks and Richard Wright. It was Algren who suggested the title *Native Son* to Wright's novel-in-progress, having discarded it himself as the title for *Somebody in Boots.* For a fuller discussion of Algren's involvement with the FWP, see Bettina Drew, *Nelson Algren: A Life on the Wild Side* (1989).

114   The publication of *Never Come Morning* was sharply opposed by Chicago's Polish community, led by the daily *Zgoda*, which saw the novel as Nazi propaganda: "It is doubtful whether Goebbels' personal adjutant could have ordered a juicier Pole-baiting tale than this Swede has dared. When free copies begin to find their way into hands of unsuspecting victims it's a signal that this anti-Polish propaganda is definitely directed by Nazi money" (quoted in *Never Come Morning,* xi).

ness" (225)—"a smoldering dump beside the Northwestern rails" (193) consisting of "abandoned hotels and boarded fences" (192).

Having grown up in this area of the city, Bruno is an active member of the local baseball team and street gang the Warriors, later to be renamed the Baldheads. But while various gang activities fill his idle days, he nevertheless feels a strong desire for better things: "I been hungry all my life, all the time [...] I never get my teeth into anythin' all my own" (32). Even his girlfriend Steffi, Bruno discovers, cannot be kept to himself, and must be shared with the gang. After a night spent at an amusement park, the young couple encounters members of Bruno's street gang on the way home, and after Bruno's sexual desires have been satisfied, the gang forms a line and proceeds to systematically rape Steffi. Powerless to interrupt the horrible scene, Bruno keeps uneasiness at bay by "feigning a toughness to himself that he could not feel" and instead concludes that "[d]ames got to get experience just like fellas" (70). Eventually overcome by the brutality of the display, Bruno takes his impotent anger out on a Greek who has entered the rape-line despite not being part of the gang from the Polish Triangle. Killing him with a kick to the jaw that causes the neck to break "like the snap of a brittle reed" (74), the sound of death can be heard by all because the usually noisy city turns quiet at the moment of violence: "There was no sound from below. There was no sound from above. As though the last El had crashed and the last trolley had finished its final run" (74). The symbolic quietness signifies that this is the defining moment of both Bruno's and Steffi's lives. Though he is not initially apprehended for the crime, Bruno has nevertheless set the same naturalistic forces in motion that eventually catch up with Wright's Bigger Thomas. As regards Steffi, the degradation causes her to drift into prostitution in Mama Tomek's brothel, where she comes to believe after a trip to church that she is "being punished justly for the sin into which her own willful frivolity had led her: 'I got only myself to blame,' she murmured" (228). This motto is repeated on a sign hanging on the wall behind the investigator when Bruno is later picked up for a smaller offense, but also questioned about the murder: "I HAVE ONLY MYSELF TO BLAME FOR

MY FALL" (81). Here, Algren's scathing critique is clear: Societal institutions such as the church and the judiciary assume no responsibility
for the actions of individuals inhabiting the opposite end of the power
structure, and they employ the rhetoric of democracy and bootstraps
ideology in order to place the blame for personal misfortune on the
unwanted elements themselves. The pretence of racial equality that
was an underlying factor in Wright's Black Chicago, therefore, has in
Algren's novel been turned into a denial of the classism that keeps the
hierarchy in place on the Polish Northwest Side.

Algren, however, much like Wright in *Lawd Today*, offers no re-
deeming qualities in his most appalling characters, and no excuses for
their crimes. The critique is implicit, not explicit, and Bruno exists
not as a symbol of oppression or deprivation, but as a human being
acting according to ability, education, environment and circumstance.
In the words of Chester E. Eisinger, Algren is "more a singer than
an explainer" (82), and while reproducing dialect and street slang, he
maintains a poetic emphasis on repetition and rhyme. For example,
when an associate of Mama Tomek hits Steffi, Algren writes: "Her
nipples and finger tips felt so cold and the room was so cold and no
room where she would be would be warm again for her ever" (244).
Language such as this is meant to represent the interiority of an uneducated mind, but it is simultaneously a highly stylized and controlled literary phrasing, suggesting the undernourished humanity
lying beneath the hardened and unsentimental surface of his characters.

Using plot only, as he has said in an interview, "to prop the book
up somehow" (Algren 1986, 301), Algren is perhaps more interested in
idiom and truthful literary expression than he is in developing a story-
line. After serving six months for robbery, Bruno tries to put things
right with Steffi and agrees to throw a title fight against a black boxer
for the neighborhood promoter. Deciding in the last minute to box
his best, Bruno wins the fight and the title, but is soon arrested for
the initial murder on charges that will likely send him to the electric
chair. Resigning himself to his fate, Bruno's final words in the novel
are: "Knew I'd never get t' be twenty-one anyhow" (284). Never reach-

ing maturity, Bruno is broken before he begins. In a symbolic image toward the end of the final fight, he notices about the referee that "the white lettering on the back of [his] red sweat shirt said simply: C H I C A G O" (275). The city itself appears as the body governing the perpetual fight between individuals on the bottom of society, and the added element of race accentuates Algren's symbolism and expands it to include ethnic minorities who battle each other for a larger share of what Chicago has to offer. The brutal reality behind this world, as Algren has Steffi notice, is that "[t]here was no horror in the quick young men, no named nor nameless horror. And in this lay the girl's own dread. In this, to Steffi, lay their greatest unnaturalness: that they spoke of the unnatural, and acted unnaturally, as though it were all so natural. For in this they became alien to her own humanness" (217). Simultaneously human and subhuman, Algren's characters exist in the horrorless slums of deceased humanity where, as the novel's title promises, "the night would be forever, the lamps would never fade, the taverns never close, morning would never come again" (223).[115]

In 1949 Algren published *The Man with the Golden Arm*, which was a popular literary sensation and the first winner of the National Book Award for fiction. Having served as a private in the Second World War, Algren's protagonist is this time a veteran who returns to the Polish ghetto with a morphine addiction brought about by shrapnel in his liver. Frankie Majcinek, known as Frankie Machine because of his machine-like ability to deal cards, is twenty-nine years old when the novel opens. He lives in a small apartment with his wife Sophie—whom he married believing she was pregnant—in the area around Damen Avenue and Division Street on the Northwest Side. Frankie's Chicago life is much like that of Bruno Biceps, and so is his implied final destination: "All had gone stale for these dis-inherited. Their very lives gave off a certain jailhouse odor: it trailed

---

115   Steffi's remark is inspired by the Russian naturalist writer Aleksandr Kuprin, from whose *Yama* (*The Pit*) (1905–1915) Algren quotes in the epigraph to the first part of *The Man with the Golden Arm*: "Do you understand, gentlemen, that all the horror is in just this—that there is no horror?" (2).

down the streets of Skid Row behind them till the city itself seemed some sort of open-roofed jail with walls for all men and laughter for very few" (17). Chicago is a prison for Algren's characters, and most of the action takes place within one building. This tenement contains Frankie's apartment, his lover Molly-O, and Antek Witwicki's Tug & Maul Bar on the ground floor, where Frankie spends most of his time. Just back from the war with a Purple Heart, Frankie celebrates with Sophie by drinking "Antek's A-Bomb Special," invented for the occasion and "made simply by pouring triple shots instead of doubles into his glasses" (67). Taking a ride to find out "what the people 'r doin' on Milwaukee" (68), Frankie crashes the car in an accident that leaves Sophie crippled. Bound to a wheelchair, Sophie uses Frankie's guilt over the accident to keep him close to her, but he eventually drifts into the arms of both Molly-O and his morphine addiction, both of which act as distractions from his monotonous and aimless life.

As was the case in *Never Come Morning*, Algren here uses plot sparingly and is instead—in true sociological fashion—primarily concerned with the accurate description of environment and behavior. The novel's treatment of drug addiction was both groundbreaking and shocking in 1949.[116] Known to Frankie as either "private McGantic" or the "monkey" he carries on his back, his addiction to morphine serves as the novel's guiding element and the catalyst for its events. Despite his successful detoxification on more than one occasion, the monotony of his card-dealing and crime-ridden life, as well as his trouble with Sophie, causes Frankie to start using again. "[T]he man on the

116   It is interesting to note that Algren started the book as a war novel set in Europe, and that drug addiction only entered the manuscript in the last draft. Its sensational treatment of addiction made it into the 1955 movie version starring Frank Sinatra, which thereby broke with the Hollywood Production Code from 1930, a code forbidding among other things the depiction of illegal drug use. Algren experienced difficulties in selling the rights to Hollywood and did not like the film, saying that both it and the novel suffered under "a presentation which confused it, in the public mind, with a cheap biography of Frank Sinatra" (2001, 94).

needle," Algren's narrative voice says, "though he be your brother, is a stranger to every human who lives without morphine" (279). Frankie's fate is sealed when he clumsily and accidentally kills his drug dealer over a poker bet. Trying as he might to evade the law, his need for a fix is more powerful than his desire to stay out of prison. The novel ends with a chase from the police, culminating when Frankie hangs himself at a cheap flophouse, unable to face either himself or the lack of morphine in prison.

In many ways a subtler novel than *Never Come Morning*, *The Man with the Golden Arm* is almost completely bereft of optimism and hope. This is in large part due to the fact that its characters are more than a decade older than the teenagers of the earlier novel and therefore harbor no illusions about their lives and status. While Bruno Biceps could still to a degree believe, along with Studs Lonigan, in the democratic American myth of equal opportunity, Frankie Machine knows that even though he can see the lights of the Loop from his fire escape—"reflected in the sky like light from some gigantic forge beating in the pit of the city's enormous heart" (281)—that part of the city is another world entirely. Identifying instead with a roach floating upside down in a jail cell water bucket, "trying dreamily to regain a foothold," Frankie "knew just how that felt" and tells it that "[y]ou ain't gettin' out till I get out" (21). The roach eventually drowns "like a sinking sub when the perpetual waters pull it downward and down forever" (25). In much the same way, Frankie is overpowered by the combined forces of environment and drug addiction, as well as by what Algren calls the "great, secret and special American guilt of owning nothing at all, in the one land where ownership and virtue are one" (17), and he slowly but steadily succumbs to the city and its "metallic moonlight's mocking glow" (98). Regarding the novel's implicit critique, James R. Giles has pointed out that "[r]epresentatives of the corrupt power structures of the city and the nation which ultimately control the fates of the urban proletariat are invisible in the novel because they are invisible to its characters" (57). With limited intellectual power, the roaches of society are doomed either to kill each other or succumb to their own vices, but are at all times kept securely at the bottom, where they are comfortably out of sight and mind of the upper classes.

In an essayistic prose poem about the city published in 1951 as *Chicago: City on the Make*, Nelson Algren takes inventory of his adopted hometown. Referring to the city as "Hustlertown" (48), he describes it in by now familiar terms as having "grown up too fast to be conscious of itself as a unified city requiring any loyalty beyond that to the American dollar" (22). The true Chicago, Algren argues, is not to be found in the Loop or in the affluent suburbs, but in the diverse and disjoined inner city neighborhoods, where "the narrow streets of the tenements seem to breathe more easily, as though closer to actual earth, than do these sinless avenues" (27). Here live the people who make a city, Algren says, and though Chicago has its problems, "once you've come to be part of this particular patch, you'll never love another. Like loving a woman with a broken nose, you may well find lovelier lovelies. But never a lovely so real" (23).

Algren's eventual problem was that the Chicago of the second half of the century was well on its way to straightening out that broken nose and lubricating its "rusty heart" (77). While he still saw the city as existing "between the curved steel of the El and the nearest Clark Street hockshop, between the penny arcade and the shooting gallery, between the basement ginmill and the biggest juke in Bronzeville" (76), that part of the city was quickly disappearing, a development causing the post mid-century Algren to be seen by many as an anachronistic proletarian or, in the words of influential critic Leslie Fiedler, a "museum piece" (43–44). As Carlo Rotella has pointed out, "Algren's literary star [...] went down with that of industrial Chicago and its characteristic types and terrains" (61) and, all but broken by bad reviews and hostile criticism, he only published intermittently over the remaining thirty years of his life, a period in which he was more famous for his failed romantic affair with French author and existentialist Simone de Beauvoir than for his literary output.[117]

---

117   For a discussion of Algren's affair with de Beauvoir, see Bettina Drew, *Nelson Algren: A Life on the Wild Side* (1989). The affair was dramatized in John

Gwendolyn Brooks

Almost immediately after she was born in Kansas in 1917, Gwendolyn Brooks and her family moved to Chicago, where she was to live her entire life. Growing up in the South Side area known as Bronzeville, she believed that "the poet should write out of his own milieu" and noted that Chicago nourished her artistically (1973, 160).[118] Brooks used the city not as theme, but instead as a backdrop for her black South Side characters in poetry and fiction, and her Bronzeville is an interesting counterpoint to Richard Wright's Black Belt. Where Wright used the city as a metaphor for white oppression, Brooks's literary Chicago consists of a black community surrounded by a white city that, in the words of Kenny J. Williams, "does not actively conspire against them; the city simply does not care" (58). While other writers of the period often sought to understand Chicago through their characters, Brooks's neighborhood regionalism is more concerned with finding meaning in the regular lives lived in the shadow of the disinterested and uncaring city.

Appearing in August 1945, at the close of the Second World War, Brooks's first collection of poetry is called *A Street in Bronzeville*, a title that announces the simultaneously specific and universal nature of its precisely observed everyday subject matter. The street could be any street in Bronzeville, and the lives portrayed are so uneventful and concerned with the details of everyday existence that the outside world is reduced to a dream rarely dreamed. In "Kitchenette Building,"

Susman's play *Nelson and Simone*, which premiered in the fall of 2000 at the Live Bait Theater in Chicago.

118   The name "Bronzeville" was coined by the Chicago *Defender*, the neighborhood's premier newspaper, and refers roughly to the area bordered by 18th Street on the north, 51st Street on the south, State Street on the west, and Cottage Grove on the east. Interchangeably known also as "Black Metropolis," the area was no longer as easily pinpointed by the early 1970s, as a comment made by Brooks in *Report From Part One* (1972), her first volume of autobiography, bears witness to: "I started out talking about Bronzeville, but Bronzeville's almost meaningless by now, I suppose, since Bronzeville has spread and spread and spread all over" (160).

for example, Brooks writes: "We are things of dry hours and the involuntary plan, / Grayed in, and gray. 'Dream' makes a giddy sound, not strong / Like 'rent,' 'feeding a wife,' 'satisfying a man'" (1971, 4). This is a world of "fried potatoes / And yesterday's garbage ripening in the hall," and where aspiration and ambition are routinely interrupted: "We wonder. But not well! not for a minute! / Since Number Five is out of the bathroom now, / We think of lukewarm water, hope to get in it" (4). Gray and lukewarm though their lives are, the characters of Brooks's poems nevertheless achieve a certain individual poignancy. By naming the poem "of De Witt Williams on his way to Lincoln Cemetery" after its generic main character, Brooks points to the individual behind the universal Bronzeville experience of street corners and dance halls, "Where he picked his women, where / He drank his liquid joy" (23). To official society, however, De Witt Williams was just another black person pouring into the rapidly expanding ghetto: "He was born in Alabama. / He was bred in Illinois. / He was nothing but a / Plain black boy" (23). Without access to the American Dream, the black characters of Bronzeville are confined by their indifferent environment, but where Wright's Bigger Thomas eventually crossed the barrier to the white world of action and self-realization, Brooks's slum dwellers will never have the opportunity to confront their oppressors. Instead, characters like "Satin-Legs Smith" live for their Sundays, where they can bathe, dress up, and parade down the street, killing time at a movie theater by admiring the heroine, "Whose ivory and yellow it is sin / For his eye to eat of" (30). Racism usually exists just under the surface in Brooks's poems and serves as a constant though rarely articulated fact of her characters' lives. By portraying implicitly the workings of segregated society, and by giving priority to the unheroic and ordinary, Brooks shifts the perspective of black Chicago writing from the socially aware protest of Wright's *Native Son* to a more variegated exploration of the complexities of individual lives—one that can exist without violence and transgression.

In 1950 Brooks became the first black writer to win the Pulitzer Prize for poetry with her second collection, *Annie Allen*, but it was in her first—and only—novel, *Maud Martha* from 1953, that she expanded significantly on the themes of *A Street in Bronzeville*. Often read autobiographically, *Maud Martha* for the most part takes place in the same neighborhood as *A Street in Bronzeville*, and consists of a series of vignettes held together by the unifying perspective of the eponymous young black girl as she grows up, marries, and has children. Here, too, racism is an important theme, but it bubbles to the surface in more prominent ways than in Brooks's earlier poems. Near the novel's beginning, importantly following her dream about an escaped gorilla, the seven-year-old Maud Martha is confronted with the seg-regated neighborhoods of the South Side: "East of Cottage Grove you saw fewer people, and those you did see had, all of them (how strange, thought Maud Martha), white faces" (1971, 135). The black part of the city literally confined by city streets, Bronzeville exists as an isolated community from where one rarely—if ever—ventures out. Following her marriage to Paul later in the novel, the young couple neverthe-less decides to go downtown for a movie. Deliberately lowering their voices to a whisper in the lobby, Paul notices that "[w]e're the only colored people here" and feels uncomfortable asking the "blonde and cold-eyed" girl at the candy counter where they should pay for their tickets (201). Maud Martha, thinking him a coward, is nevertheless aware that "[t]he people in the lobby tried to avoid looking curiously at two shy Negroes wanting desperately not to seem shy" (202). Here, as in Brooks's Bronzeville poems, the expected confrontation with white society is omitted, as the couple is instead let into the theater, where they enjoy the movie. But their aspiration to equality only lasts as long as the lights are dim:

> When the picture was over, and the lights revealed them for what they were, the Negroes stood up among the furs and good cloth and faint perfume, looked about them eagerly. They hoped they would meet no cruel eyes. They hoped no one would look intruded upon. They had enjoyed the picture so, they were so happy, they wanted to laugh, to say warmly to the other outgoers, 'Good, huh? Wasn't it swell?'

This, of course, they could not do. But if only no one would look
intruded upon.... (204).

Maud Martha experiences several similar encounters with white society. Taking her young daughter to see Santa Claus at a downtown
department store, she finds that "[h]e was unable to see either mother
or child" (299). Invisible among the city's whites, Maud Martha is
incapable of explanation when her daughter asks "[w]hy didn't Santa
Claus like me?" (300) and yearns to "jerk trimming scissors from
purse and jab jab jab that evading eye" (301). Her initially violent impulse, however, is soon extinguished: "She could neither resolve nor
dismiss. There were these scraps of baffled hate in her, hate with no
eyes, no smile and—this she especially regretted, called her hungriest
lack—not much voice" (302). Like the *Bronzeville* characters waiting
for lukewarm water, Maud Martha is powerless before the racism
pervading society and instead focuses her energy inward—on herself
and her family.

Going to work in the kitchen of a wealthy white woman, Maud
Martha is told to "always use the back entrance" (284). After her first
day of being treated by Mrs. Burns-Cooper "[a]s though she were a
child, a ridiculous one, and one that ought to be given a little shaking"
(288), she decides to leave her new job: "Why, one was a human being.
One wore clean nightgowns. One loved one's baby. One drank cocoa
by the fire—or the gas range—come the evening, in the wintertime"
(289). Asserting her equality by refusing to be treated as inferior because she is black, Maud Martha has found the only possible way for
her to oppose racist society. Not undergoing a search for identity on
the tragic scale of Wright's Bigger Thomas, Maud Martha instead
affirms her humanity on a smaller stage. Where *Native Son* begins
with Bigger symbolically killing a rat, Maud Martha spares the life
of a trapped mouse and learns, as critics Patricia and Vernon Lattin
have noted, that "she can in her own fashion create value and meaning" (143). Where Bigger is executed by the law, Maud Martha asks
near the end of the novel: "What, *what*, am I to do with all of this
life?" (304), a comment referring to the limited opportunities of a

black woman in Chicago's Bronzeville, but also, on a more optimistic note, an affirmation of the life she has created for herself by looking inward, instead of outward, for a solution to her problems. Beverly Guy-Sheftall has argued that Brooks's "sexual identity as well as her racial identity has molded her vision of the city" (233), and the novel certainly offers a peaceful alternative to *Native Son*'s male fantasies of power and violent confrontation.

Grounded in the reality of ghetto life, Brooks's poems and novel tell the stories of characters living on the margins of society, a position that is of course arbitrary and therefore made central by any expression of individual experience. The white man's margin, in other words, is the black man's reality, and by providing her everyday characters with a distinctive poetic voice, Brooks insists on their common but nevertheless fundamental humanity. As Brooks scholar Maria K. Mootry has pointed out, *A Street in Bronzeville*—and to a lesser degree *Maud Martha*—is located in the space between European modernism and the populist Chicago tradition of Carl Sandburg and Edgar Lee Masters.[119] Following the death of Sandburg, Brooks appropriately became the new poet laureate of Illinois in 1968 and continued to be so until her death in 2000, all the while publishing frequently and with great success.

Saul Bellow

One character in Chicago fiction who is always aware of himself and his environment is the titular character of Saul Bellow's *The Adventures of Augie March* from 1953. Bellow was born in Canada in 1915 to Russian Jewish immigrants, but moved as a child with his family to Chicago. Inspired perhaps by Bellow's own role as outsider in the city as well as in American society, Augie, the narrator, begins the book about his life by positively affirming:

---

119   Mootry makes the compelling argument in "'Down the Whirlwind of Good Rage': An Introduction to Gwendolyn Brooks" (1987).

I am an American, Chicago born—Chicago that somber city—and go at things as I have taught myself, free-style, and will make the record in my own way: first to knock, first admitted; sometimes an innocent knock, sometimes a not so innocent. But a man's character is his fate, says Heraclitus, and in the end there isn't any way to disguise the nature of the knocks by acoustical work on the door or by gloving the knuckles (3).

Refusing from the outset to let his immigrant roots and immediate environment of Chicago's slums get in the way of greatness, Augie approaches life, as Christopher Hitchens has observed, "seeking no one's permission and deferring to no idea of limitation. His making, like his omnivorous education, will be his own."[120] Equal parts traditional *Bildungsroman* and contemporary picaresque adventure novel, *The Adventures of Augie March* takes its beginning in Chicago's predominantly Jewish Humboldt Park neighborhood, following its charming and rambling protagonist from the 1920s up until the early 1950s, ending with Augie sitting in a sidewalk café in Paris, a true American and a man of the world. Growing up poor on the streets of Chicago, Augie is brought into contact with an impressive panorama of eccentric characters, the first being his adopted Grandma Lausch, who teaches him to lie to the social services and who rules the household and his dim mother with an iron fist. Perhaps the most important influence, however, is the crippled Einhorn, owner of the local pool room and described by Augie as worthy of comparison to Caesar, Machiavelli and Ulysses. Einhorn warns him that "[y]oung fellows brought up in bad luck, like you, are naturals to keep the jails filled—the reformatories, all the institutions. What the state orders bread and beans long in advance for. It knows there's an element that can be depended on to come behind bars to eat it" (117). A few sentences later he continues: "In the end you can't save your soul and

120   Quoted in Hitchens's introduction to the 2001 Penguin Books edition of *The Adventures of Augie March*, viii.

life by thought. But if you *think*, the least of the consolation prizes is the world" (117).

Though spending his time working various jobs—as dog stylist, boxing promoter, labor organizer and contract book thief, to name a few—Augie nevertheless heeds Einhorn's advice of thinking his way through life. Placing himself and his surroundings in a perspective of cultural knowledge and experience, he is the American Adam with a historical context, exemplified by his description of a trip back to Chicago from Michigan:

> If you've seen a winter London open thundering mouth in its awful last minutes of river light or have come with cold clanks from the Alps into Torino in December white steam then you've known like greatness of place. Thirty crowded miles on oil-spotted road, where the furnace, gas and machine volcanoes cooked the Empedocles fundamentals into pig iron, girders and rails; another ten miles of loose city, five of tight—the tenements—and we got off the trailer not far from the Loop and went into Thompson's for a stew and spaghetti meal (90–91).[121]

Invoking in short succession everything from the London of Charles Dickens to the philosophy of Greco-Roman antiquity, and ending the passage in a Chicago restaurant, Augie defines his own existence in terms larger than the circumstances he is born into, drawing a straight line from the collected pool of human history to himself and enthusiastically asking: "What did Danton lose his head for, or why was there a Napoleon, if it wasn't to make a nobility of us all?" (29).[122]

---

121   The Loop is the downtown business area of Chicago, so called because the elevated railroad—the El—makes a loop around it on its way through the city.

122   Augie's ability to draw on ancient myths as well as world history might come from Bellow's childhood of speaking Yiddish with his family. James Atlas, in his exemplary *Bellow: A Biography* (2000), quotes from Bellow himself: "The most ordinary Yiddish conversation is full of the grandest historical, mythologi-

Similarly, looking at Chicago from a tall building upon one of his many returns to the city, he muses: "Well, here it was again, westward from this window, the gray snarled city with the hard black straps of rails, enormous industry cooking and its vapor shuddering to the air, the climb and fall of its stages in construction or demolition like mesas, and on these the different powers and sub-powers crouched like sphinxes" (425). In passages such as these, Chicago becomes a city of almost mythical stature, linked with grandiose nature and ancient Egypt in a single sentence, while at the same time retaining its distinctiveness as the industrial world's most modern city.[123] As writer Joyce Carol Oates has said, in the novel "Chicago is America writ large" (21). But America, in turn, is also the world writ large, in the center of which, and unabashed to be there, is Augie March. A seeker born, as he says, under "the sign of the recruit" (508), Augie is easily influenced by others, and he changes jobs, cities and countries with increasing regularity, looking for meaning and what literary historians Richard Ruland and Malcolm Bradbury have called the "transcendental adventure" that he believes to be his fate (378). Refusing both the disappointed life and his tendency to be shaped by others, he prompts the reader in the novel's closing words: "Look at me, going everywhere! Why, I am a sort of Columbus of those near-at-hand and believe you can come to them in this immediate *terra incognito* that spreads out in every gaze. I may well be a flop at this line of endeavor. Columbus too thought he was a flop, probably,

---

cal, and religious allusions. The Creation, the fall, the flood, Egypt, Alexander, Titus, Napoleon, the Rothschilds, the Sages, and the Laws may get into the discussion of an egg, a clothes-line, or a pair of pants" (14).

123   Bellow, in a 1973 *Publisher's Weekly* interview with Joyce Illig, said of the extreme modernity of Chicago: "In Chicago, things were done for the first time, which the rest of the world later learned and imitated. Capitalist production was pioneered in the stockyards, in refrigerator cars, in the creation of the Pullman, in the creation of farm machinery, and with it also certain urban political phenomena which are associated with the new condition of modern democracy. All that happened here. It happened early" (110).

when they sent him back in chains. Which didn't prove there was no America" (536).

Sprawling, fresh and freewheeling, *The Adventures of Augie March* is, as literary critic Steven Marcus has said, Bellow's "love song to America and to the range of urban experience in his native Chicago" (235). On a larger scale, it represents a crossroads for Chicago literature and a feeling of simultaneously having reached the end of one line and the beginning of another. With *The Adventures of Augie March*, Chicago fiction, and the characters inhabiting its best novels, frees itself from the environment, so to speak, and finally declines to be at the mercy of external forces. Taking charge of his own destiny, Augie symbolically completes the quest begun sixty years earlier of comprehending the nature of the city. Chicago, Augie concludes, can only be understood—along with himself—in terms combining and transcending the whole of the world's accumulated history. He thus says one New Year's morning while looking out at Lake Michigan, "[t]he days have not changed though the times have. The sailors who first saw America, that sweet sight, where the belly of the ocean had brought them, didn't see more beautiful color than this" (283). Chicago is America and America is the world. And Augie—of course—is both of them combined.

_5_
Beyond the Tradition
Perspectives in Chicago
Literature since 1953

As exemplified by the fiction of Farrell, Wright, Algren, Brooks and Bellow, Chicago in the first half of the twentieth century was a city consisting of several distinct neighborhoods. As journalist Mike Royko writes in *Boss*, his 1971 biographical exposure of the city's legendary mayor Richard J. Daley: "Chicago, until as late as the 1950s, was a place where people stayed put for a while, creating tightly knit neighborhoods, as small-townish as any village in the wheat fields" (30).[124] But "because of the car, the shifting society, and the suburban sprawl" (30), Royko explains, this is no longer so. As the 1933 World's Fair and its official slogan "A Century of Progress" proclaimed, Chicago continued to be a city on the make, where nothing stayed the same for very long.

With the rapid decline of the meatpacking business in the 1960s and the eventual closure of the last of the stockyards in 1971, Chicago lost more than a business—it lost a big part of its identity. And because Chicago had always been a place dominated by larger-than-life businessmen and multitudes of blue-collar workers and shopkeepers,

---

124   Richard J. Daley from the city's Irish Bridgeport neighborhood served five terms as mayor of Chicago from 1955 until his death in 1976. Known as "The Boss," Daley's many grand-scale public projects helped revitalize Chicago, but earned him a reputation of being brutish, racist and corrupt, thanks in large part to Royko's exposé.

the shift in American business away from family-owned companies and toward anonymous corporations changed the face of the city forever. And among the first things to go were the old-fashioned ethnic neighborhoods. In Saul Bellow's novel *Humboldt's Gift* from 1975, the narrator Charlie Citrine pointedly takes a nostalgic cab ride through his old Polish neighborhood:

> A whole block had gone down. Lovi's Hungarian Restaurant had been swept away, plus Ben's Pool Hall and the old brick carbarn and Gratch's Funeral Parlor, out of which both my parents had been buried. Eternity got no picturesque interval here. The ruins of time had been bulldozed, scraped, loaded in trucks, and dumped as fill. New steel beams were going up. Polish kielbasa no longer hung in butchers' windows. The sausages in the *carnicería* were Caribbean, purple and wrinkled. The old shop signs were gone. The new ones said HOY. MUDANZAS. IGLESIA (75).

In some ways Bellow describes the business-as-usual of Chicago, yet the destruction of the old neighborhoods and the changing realities of the city produced another significant departure for Chicago literature. To the earliest generations of writers, Chicago had offered such new and unifying symbols as the skyscraper, the World's Columbian Exposition, and the specter of burgeoning industrial capitalism, but the city's newer incarnations offered little in the way of such thematic unity. And where post-Depression writers had looked to their neighborhoods for the coherence missing from the city at large, the writers working after the 1950s conceived of both the city and its neighborhoods as fragments.

While Chicago literature gradually moved away from attempts to thematically capture the essence of the city or of a specific neighborhood, this lack of coherence has also manifested itself formally in much of this period's best Chicago writing. In "The Writer in Chicago," a roundtable discussion by Maxine Chernoff, Cyrus Colter, Stuart Dybek, Reginald Gibbons and Fred Shafer published in *TriQuarterly* magazine in 1984, Gibbons asks the first three, who have all written short-story collections, whether "the appeal of the story form to all three of you as city dwellers isn't partly because one of the things you wished to memorialize [...] is not the great sweep of intertwined relationships of a novel, but the fact that there are so many things going on that have no connection whatsoever" (339). All three writers agree, and their work illustrates the point further.

Colter was born in 1910 but only published his first book, *The Beach Umbrella*, in 1970. It is a collection of fourteen stories about black Chicago. Set partly on the South Side and partly in other locations around the city, the stories depict lives and events from all layers of black society, and do so with a breadth rarely attempted in black Chicago literature. Colter's characters are often faced with circumstances threatening to change their lives, and despite a predominance of wretched old widowers, drug-addicts and abused wives, he also portrays the black middle and upper classes in several stories, and does so with equal power and clarity. Inspired by James Joyce's *Dubliners*, Colter's collection, as critic James Hurt has pointed out, "has an overall design, rather than being a random collection" (106). This design, however, has little to do with unity of theme, and is instead a simple juxtaposition of stories with widely varying concerns next to each other, creating in the reader the impression of having witnessed a series of snapshots documenting fragments of black Chicago experience in 1970. While set firmly in Chicago and abounding in references to specific locations, there is little in *The Beach Umbrella* that is *about* Chicago in the same way, for example, as Henry B. Fuller's *With the Procession*. Part of the explanation, perhaps, is that times have finally caught up with Chicago, and that its 1970 incarnation is no longer unique in American experience. Its inhabitants have grown up with the city, and because they are better able to understand and therefore—like Augie March—transcend their environment, Colter's black city dwellers go about their daily lives without a heightened awareness of the city's power and significance. Colter himself, in the *TriQuarterly* roundtable discussion, talks about his decision to write about black Chicago: "[L]ike the race of the character, I've also chosen Chicago because it was natural and convenient—because I've convinced myself, rightly or not, that they are more familiar to me" (326–327). Colter's characters, he says, "happen to be Chicagoans, and I think there is something unique in the fact that they do live in Chicago" (327), but maybe, he soon admits, "it's my imagination that thinks it's unique" (328). While a far cry from the strong sense of place in Richard Wright's Chicago novels, and even further from Robert Herrick's intense statements about the city, Colter's sentiments and literary strategy are surprisingly representative of his generation of writers.

In *Bop* from 1986, Maxine Chernoff takes a similar approach. While Chicago remains a presence in most of the short stories, its function is more that of an atmospheric backdrop—"The Hancock building was shrouded in clouds of smoke or fog" (46)—than of a condition to be dealt with by her characters. In the title story, for example, the newly immigrated Oleg visits Lake Michigan, but the narrative—in which he befriends a young girl, meets her mother, and finds an abandoned baby on the beach, all of which conspire to taunt him with the possibility of starting a family—could have played out with little variation in almost any major American city. In the *TriQuarterly* discussion, Chernoff explains about setting her fiction in Chicago: "If this is going to be a place for you, part of the place will be your neighborhood, your environs, the relatives who are as much landscape for you as buildings are" (326). Echoing Colter's sentiments of convenience, Chernoff also shifts the focus to the people inhabiting Chicago. No longer a naturalistic megapolis, the city in Chernoff's stories is conceived in terms of the people living in it and their interactions with each other.

Of the three writers participating in the roundtable discussion, Stuart Dybek's collection *The Coast of Chicago* from 1990 bears the closest resemblance to earlier Chicago writing, and does so because it is rooted firmly in the 1950s South Side neighborhood in which he grew up. Carlo Rotella has argued that "Dybek both engages with the ghost of Nelson Algren's Chicago and lays it to rest" (108), and while Dybek's stories—like Algren's—are often concerned with the lives of young people growing up on the neighborhood streets, his characters soon become alienated from the city itself by the changes taking place around them: "It was hard to believe there ever were streetcars. The city back then, the city of their fathers, which was as far back as a family memory extended, even the city of their childhoods, seemed as remote to Eddie and Manny as the capital of some foreign country. The past collapsed about them—decayed, bulldozed, obliterated" (130). This city of their fathers is the city of Algren, and it is fitting that Dybek was born in 1942, the year Algren's *Never Come Morning* was published. But while Algren's literary influence is evident throughout *The Coast of Chicago*, Dybek's multiethnic neighborhood is a generation removed from the largely Polish world of Frankie Machine. Hispanic and black characters make appearances in Dybek's neighborhood, and at the end of "Blight," one of the collection's strongest stories, Dave, the narrator, looks around and reports, like Bellow's Charlie Citrine, that "[t]he neighborhood was mostly Mexican now, with many of the signs over the stores in Spanish, but the bars were still called the Edelweiss Tap and the Budweiser Lounge" (70). This disconnection between the past and the present is characteristic of Chicago's post-1950s resistance to cohesive statements and sweeping generalizations. No longer consisting of unambiguous parts and monoethnic neighborhoods, the centered city had vanished. And where earlier Chicagoans attempted to find meaning in the city itself, Dybek's characters look, like Eddie in "Hot Ice," to the fragmented transparency of its windows: "He would see a window from a bus, like the Greek butcher shop on Halsted with its pyramid of lamb skulls, and make a mental photograph of it. He had special windows all over the city. It was how he held the city together in his mind" (146). As people moved out of the neighborhoods, then, so did literature. And while writers such as Bellow and Dybek nostalgically attempted to come to terms with the disappearance of the old city, other writers such as Colter and Chernoff followed Chicago into its new and somewhat generic present incarnation.

Nelson Algren wrote in 1963 that Chicago was no longer the Second City, it was "The Secondhand City" (270), and while the main currents in post-1950s Chicago literature have been concerned with the destruction of the old neighborhoods and the appearance of a new and thematically decentralized city, some writers have continued many of the traditions begun in the late nineteenth century. Where Dybek, as outlined, has continued Algren's exploration of neighborhood youth, the playwright David Mamet, in plays like *Sexual Perversion in Chicago* (1974) and *American Buffalo* (1975), uses his ear for dialogue to revitalize Algren's—and, to a certain extent, George Ade's—attempts to represent character through the popular language of Chicagoese. Likewise, the widely syndicated Mike Royko has continued the tradition of the popular newspaper column, which was first invented by Chicago writers like Ade and Eugene Field. For several decades until his death in 1997, Royko's columns were written first for the *Daily News* of Field's best work, and later for both the *Sun-Times* and the *Tribune*, the city's two remaining dailies. Historian Studs Terkel, taking his name from James T. Farrell's seminal novels, has continued the tradition of listening to the concerns of regular people in books such as *Division Street: America* from 1967, and he attempts to make sense of the city as a whole in his short but rambling *Chicago* from 1986, which mixes popular history with personal recollection and old-fashioned boosterism. What all of these have in common is a continued preoccupation, in the face of a changing urban environment, with the things that have made Chicago literature what it is, along with a desire to continue a tradition that has helped shape American literature as a whole.

Another development is an apparent renewal of the fascination with the World's Columbian Exposition, which has recently served as material for both historians and writers of fiction, and has done so across multiple artistic genres. In *The Devil in the White City*, his successful and engrossing volume of popular history from 2003, Erik Larson juxtaposes architect Daniel Burnham and the grandiosity of the fair with the brutal contemporary killings by H. H. Holmes, whom he alleges to be America's first serial killer. Meticulously researched and entertainingly written, Larson's book does a good job of conveying the two metaphorically different sides of Chicago in 1893, and it was a surprising but deserved bestseller. A strikingly similar approach is taken in first-time author Alec Michod's novel *The White City* from 2004, which describes a woman detective solving the fictional murders of a killer operating at the fair. The World's Columbian Exposition also serves as an important thematic backdrop in Chris Ware's multi-generational graphic novel *Jimmy Corrigan: The Smartest Kid on Earth*. Chronicling the lives of the almost exclusively male members of a Chicago family from the 1890s to the present day, the novel uses the fair as a metaphor for parental neglect and dreams unfulfilled. In some ways a definitive Chicago novel, *Jimmy Corrigan* weaves a rich tapestry of the city's history and shows through the use of words and images how its characters' lives are interconnected across time and place. The renewed fascination with the fair has also manifested itself in music, where Michigan-born singer-songwriter Sufjan Stevens has released two albums of symphonic chamber-pop inspired by Illinois in general and by Chicago in particular. *Illinois* from 2005, along with its 2006 companion-piece of studio outtakes called *The Avalanche*, is part of Stevens's ongoing project of recording an album for every state in the union. Using the World's Columbian Exposition as their thematic centerpiece, the albums also include song-poems about Saul Bellow and Jane Addams, and about being visited by the ghost of Carl Sandburg, who symbolically asks Stevens: "Are you writing from the heart?" Sandburg, of course, was writing from both his own heart and from the heart of the city itself, and while a group of writers have recently rediscovered the magic and symbolic promise of the fair, the multifaceted heart of the modern city has also received attention.

Being a "Chicago writer," contemporary author Adam Langer has said, "almost sounds like something out of a different era, like owning a Studebaker or having played for the Brooklyn Dodgers," and while no such firm category can be said to exist today, a new multiethnic literature is making its mark on the city (quoted in McNamee, 1). Writers of Hispanic descent such as Sandra Cisneros, Ana Castillo and Pulitzer Prize-nominated Luis Urrea have written about their experiences in the traditionally European neighborhoods of Chicago, and Bosnian refugee Aleksandar Hemon—who came to

America in 1992—became a minor sensation with the publication in 2000 of *The Question of Bruno*, a collection of short stories about his experiences in Chicago. With the appearance of such a diverse range of talent, Chicago literature has taken a big step into the twenty-first century—and toward becoming as eclectic as the contemporary city itself. And while today's writers are perhaps not as conscious of their Chicago heritage as their literary predecessors, the city nevertheless continues its work behind the scenes. As Daniela Kuper, the author of the Jewish-themed novel *Hunger and Thirst* from 2004, has said about the city: "It's my core, it made me. I can't walk away from it anymore than I can voluntarily leave my left leg. And when I try, the page goes dead. If you take Chicago out of my book, there is no book" (quoted in McNamee, 1).

Accordingly, while Studs Terkel once claimed that the city had "been molded by the muscle rather than the word" (11), the word has also been molded by Chicago's muscle. It is this tension that lies at the center of the Chicago Tradition. "[P]art civilized, part barbarians, part triumphant, and part ravaged," declares Saul Bellow: "This is our condition, Chicago's condition, and our American condition" (quoted in Raymer, 382).

Bibliography

Adams, Henry. *The Education of Henry Adams* [1907], ed. Ernest Samuels (Boston: Houghton Mifflin, 1973).

Addams, Jane. *The Second Twenty Years at Hull-House* (New York: Macmillan, 1930).

——. *Twenty Years at Hull-House: With Autobiographical Notes* [1910] (New York: Signet Classic, 1961).

Ade, George. *Artie and Pink Marsh: Two Novels by George Ade* [*Artie*: 1896, *Pink Marsh*: 1897] (Chicago: University of Chicago Press, 1963).

——. *Chicago Stories*, ed. Franklin J. Meine (Chicago: Henry Regnery, 1963).

——. *The Permanent Ade: The Living Writings of George Ade*, ed. Fred C. Kelly (Indianapolis: Bobbs-Merrill, 1947).

Alexander, William. "The Limited American, the Great Loneliness, and the Singing Fire: Carl Sandburg's 'Chicago Poems.'" *American Literature* 45.1 (1973): 67–83.

Algren, Nelson. *Chicago: City on the Make* [1951] (Chicago: University of Chicago Press, 2001).

——. *The Man with the Golden Arm* [1949] (Garden City, NY: Doubleday, 1950).

——. *The Neon Wilderness* [1947] (New York: Four Walls Eight Windows, 1986).

——. *Never Come Morning* [1942] (New York: Four Walls Eight Windows, 1987).

——. *Who Lost an American?* (New York: Macmillan, 1963).

Anderson, David D. "The Chicago Renaissance in Fiction." *Midwestern Miscellany* 27.2 (1999): 7–16.

——. "Dispersion and Direction: Sherwood Anderson, the Chicago Renaissance, and the American Mainstream." In *Midamerica V: The Yearbook of the Society for the Study of Midwestern Literature*, ed. David D. Anderson (East Lansing, MI: Midwestern Press, 1978), 66–75.

——. *Sherwood Anderson: An Introduction and Interpretation* (New York: Barnes and Noble, 1967).

——. "Sherwood Anderson, Henry Blake Fuller, James T. Farrell, and the Midwestern City as Metaphor and Reality." *SSML Newsletter: The Society for the Study of Midwestern Literature* 25.3 (1995): 16–21.

Anderson, Sherwood. *Letters of Sherwood Anderson*, ed. Howard Mumford Jones and Walter B. Rideout (Boston: Little, Brown, 1953).

———. *Marching Men: A Critical Text* [*Marching Men*: 1917], ed. Ray Lewis White (Cleveland: Press of Case Western Reserve University, 1972).

———. "The New Note." *The Little Review Anthology*, ed. Margaret Anderson (New York: Hermitage House, 1953), 13–15.

———. *Poor White* [1920] (New York: Viking, 1973).

———. *Sherwood Anderson's Memoirs: A Critical Edition* [*Sherwood Anderson's Memoirs*: 1942], ed. Ray Lewis White (Chapel Hill: University of North Carolina Press, 1969).

———. *A Story Teller's Story: The tale of an American writer's journey through his own imaginative world and through the world of facts, with many of the experiences and impressions among other writers—told in many notes—in four books—and an Epilogue* (New York: B. W. Huebsch, 1924).

———. "When I Left Business for Literature." *Century Magazine* 108.4 (1924): 489–496.

———. *Windy McPherson's Son* [1916] (London: Jonathan Cape, 1923).

———. *Winesburg, Ohio* [1919] (New York: Dover, 1995).

Atlas, James. *Bellow: A Biography* (New York: Random House, 2000).

Avrich, Paul. *The Haymarket Tragedy* (Princeton, NJ: Princeton University Press, 1984).

Bander, Edward J. *Mr. Dooley and Mr. Dunne: The Literary Life of a Chicago Catholic* (Charlottesville, VI: Michie Company Law Publishers, 1981).

Baraka, Amiri. "Black Literature and the Afro-American Nation: The Urban Voice." In *Literature and the American Urban Experience: Essays on the City and Literature*, ed. Michael C. Jaye and Ann Chalmers Watts (Manchester: Manchester University Press, 1981), 139–159.

Bellow, Saul. *The Adventures of Augie March* [1953]. Introduction by Christopher Hitchens (London: Penguin, 2001).

———. *Humboldt's Gift* (New York: Viking, 1975).

Bender, Thomas. *Toward an Urban Vision: Ideas and Institutions in Nineteenth-Century America* (Lexington: University Press of Kentucky, 1975).

Berthoff, Warner. *The Ferment of Realism: American Literature, 1884–1919* (New York: Free Press, 1965).

Botkin, B. A. "WPA and Folklore Research: 'Bread and Song.'" *Southern Folklore Quarterly* 3.1 (1939): 7–14.

Bowron, Bernard R., Jr. *Henry B. Fuller of Chicago: The Ordeal of a Genteel Realist in Ungenteel America* (Westport, CT: Greenwood Press, 1974).

Boyesen, Hjalmar Hjort. "In the World of Art and Letters: The Cliff-Dwellers." *Cosmopolitan Magazine* XVL (1894): 373–374.

Bradbury, Malcolm. "The Cities of Modernism." In *Modernism: 1890–1930* [1976], ed. Malcolm Bradbury and James McFarlane (London: Penguin, 1991), 96–104.

———. *The Modern American Novel: New Edition* (New York: Viking, 1993).

Bray, Robert C. *Rediscoveries: Literature and Place in Illinois* (Urbana: University of Illinois Press, 1982).

Briggs, Asa. *Victorian Cities* [1963] (Long Acre, London: Odhams, 1965).

Brooks, Gwendolyn. *Report From Part One* (Detroit: Broadside Press, 1972).

———. *The World of Gwendolyn Brooks: A Street in Bronzeville* [1945]; *Annie Allen* [1949]; *Maud Martha* [1953]; *The Bean Eaters* [1960]; *In the Mecca* [1968] (New York: Harper & Row, 1971).

Brooks, Van Wyck. *The Confident Years: 1885–1915* (New York: E. P. Dutton, 1952).

Buck, Lillie West Brown. *Amy Leslie at the Fair* (Chicago: W. B. Conkey, 1893).

Butler, Robert. "Farrell's Ethnic Neighborhood and Wright's Urban Ghetto: Two Visions of Chicago's South Side." *Melus* 18.1 (1993): 103–111.

Cappetti, Carla. *Writing Chicago: Modernism, Ethnography, and the Novel* (New York: Columbia University Press, 1993).

"Carl Sandburg." In *The Norton Anthology of American Literature.* Shorter Fifth Edition, ed. Nina Baym (New York: W. W. Norton, 1999), 1885–1886.

Cather, Willa. *Lucy Gayheart* (New York: Alfred A. Knopf, 1935).

———. *The Song of the Lark* [1915] (Boston: Houghton Mifflin, 1937).

———. *The World and the Parish: Willa Cather's Articles and Reviews, 1893–1902.* Volume Two, ed. William M. Curtin (Lincoln: University of Nebraska Press, 1970).

Chamberlin, Everett. *Chicago and Its Suburbs* (Chicago: Hungerford, 1874).

Chernoff, Maxine. *Bop* (Minneapolis: Coffee House Press, 1986).

———, Cyrus Colter, Stuart Dybek, Reginald Gibbons and Fred Shafer. "The Writer in Chicago: A Roundtable." *TriQuarterly* 60 (1984): 325–347.

Costello, Brannon. "Richard Wright's *Lawd Today!* and the Political Uses of Modernism." *African American Review* 37.1 (2003): 39–52.

Couser, G. Thomas. "Art in Chicago: Fuller's *With the Procession.*" *American Literary Realism, 1870–1910* 13.1 (1980): 31–40.

Cowan, Michael H. *City of the West: Emerson, America, and Urban Metaphor* (New Haven: Yale University Press, 1967).

Cowley, Malcolm. "Chicago Poem." *New Republic* 106.18 (1942): 614.

Crevecœur, J. Hector St. John de. *Letters from an American Farmer* [1782] (New York: Everyman's Library, 1971).

Cronon, William. *Nature's Metropolis: Chicago and the Great West* (New York: W. W. Norton, 1991).

Cunliffe, Marcus. *The Literature of the United States*. Fourth Edition (London: Penguin, 1987).

Day, Robert A. "The Birth and Death of a Satirist: Eugene Field and Chicago's Growing Pains." *American Literature* 22.4 (1951): 466–478.

Dedmon, Emmett. *Fabulous Chicago* (London: Hamish Hamilton, 1953).

Dell, Floyd. *The Briary-Bush* (New York: Alfred A. Knopf, 1921).

——. "Chicago in Fiction" [in two parts]. *Bookman* XXXVIII (November 1913): 270–277; (December 1913): 375–379.

——. *Moon-Calf* [1920] (London: William Heinemann, 1922).

Dreiser, Theodore. *Dawn* (New York: Horace Liveright, 1931).

——. *The "Genius"* [1915] (New York: Horace Liveright, 1931).

——. "The Great American Novel." *American Spectator* 1.2 (1932): 1.

——. *Newspaper Days* [1922] (New York: Horace Liveright, 1931).

——. *Sister Carrie* [1900]. Introduction by E. L. Doctorow (New York: Bantam, 1992).

——. *Trilogy of Desire: The Financier* [1912]; *The Titan* [1914]; *The Stoic* [1947] (New York: World Publishing, 1972).

Drew, Bettina. *Nelson Algren: A Life on the Wild Side* (New York: G. P. Putnam's Sons, 1989).

Duffey, Bernard. *The Chicago Renaissance in American Letters: A Critical History* (East Lansing: The Michigan State College Press, 1954).

Duncan, Hugh Dalziel. *Culture and Democracy: The Struggle for Form in Society and Architecture in Chicago and the Middle West during the Life and Times of Louis H. Sullivan* (Totowa, NJ: The Bedminster Press, 1965).

——. *The Rise of Chicago as a Literary Center from 1885 to 1920: A Sociological Essay in American Culture* (Totowa, NJ: The Bedminster Press, 1964).

Dunne, Finley Peter. *Mr. Dooley's Philosophy* (New York: Robert Howard Russell, 1900).

Dybek, Stuart. *The Coast of Chicago* (New York: Alfred A. Knopf, 1990).

——. Introduction to *Chicago Stories: Tales of the City*, ed. John Miller (San Francisco: Chronicle, 1993), xi–xiii.

Eisinger, Chester E. *Fiction of the Forties* (Chicago: University of Chicago Press, 1963).

Emerson, Ralph Waldo. "The American Scholar." In *The Norton Anthology of American Literature*. Shorter Fifth Edition, ed. Nina Baym (New York: W. W. Norton, 1999), 525–538.

——. *Essays, Second Series* [1844] (Rockville, MD: Arc Manor, 2007).

———. *The Journals of Ralph Waldo Emerson*. Volume 10, ed. Edward Waldo Emerson and Waldo Emerson Forbes (Boston: Houghton Mifflin, 1914).

Esteve, Mary. *The Aesthetics and Politics of the Crowd in American Literature* (Cambridge: Cambridge University Press, 2003).

"Eugene Field's Death." *Overland Monthly* 26.156 (1895): 672–673.

Farrell, James T. *The League of Frightened Philistines: And Other Papers* (New York: Vanguard Press, 1945).

———. *Studs Lonigan* [*Young Lonigan*: 1932, *The Young Manhood of Studs Lonigan*: 1934, *Judgment Day*: 1935] (London: Granada, 1979).

Ferlazzo, Paul J. "The Urban-Rural Vision of Carl Sandburg." In *Midamerica I: The Yearbook of the Society for the Study of Midwestern Literature*, ed. David D. Anderson (East Lansing, MI: Midwestern Press, 1974), 52–57.

Fiedler, Leslie. "The Noble Savages of Skid Row." *The Reporter* 15 (1956): 43–44.

Field, Eugene. *Culture's Garland: Being Memoranda of The Gradual Rise of Literature, Art, Music and Society in Chicago, and other Western Ganglia* (Boston: Ticknor, 1887).

———. *The Eugene Field Book: Verses, Stories, and Letters for School Reading* [1898], ed. Mary E. Burt and Mary B. Cable (Freeport, NY: Books for Libraries Press, 1969).

———. *The House: An Episode in the Lives of Reuben Baker, Astronomer, and of his Wife Alice* (New York: Charles Scribner's Sons, 1896).

———. *The Works of Eugene Field: Sharps and Flats I*. Volume XI, ed. Slason Thompson (New York: Charles Scribner's Sons, 1901).

Fitzgerald, F. Scott. *The Crack-Up: With other Uncollected Pieces, Note-Books and Unpublished Letters; Together with Letters to Fitzgerald from Gertrude Stein, Edith Wharton, T. S. Eliot, Thomas Wolfe and John Dos Passos; And Essays and Poems by Paul Rosenfeld, Glenway Wescott, John Dos Passos, John Peale Bishop and Edmund Wilson* [1945], ed. Edmund Wilson (New York: New Directions, 1956).

Flanagan, John T. "Hamlin Garland Writes to his Chicago Publisher." *American Literature* 23.4 (1952): 447–457.

———. "Theodore Dreiser's Chicago." *Revue des langues vivantes* XXXII (1966): 131–144.

Frank, Waldo. "The Land of the Pioneer" [1919]. In *Critics of Culture: Literature and Society in the Early Twentieth Century*, ed. Alan Trachtenberg (New York: John Wiley & Sons, 1976), 119–144.

Fuller, Henry B. "Art in America." *Bookman* X (1899): 218–224.

———. "The Ballade of the Bank-Teller." *Puck Magazine* 9 (September 1881): 451.

———. *Bertram Copes's Year* [1919]. Afterword by Andrew Solomon (New York: Turtle Point, 1998).

———. *The Cliff-Dwellers: A Novel* [1893] (Ridgewood, NJ: Gregg Press, 1968).

———. *On the Stairs* (Boston: Houghton Mifflin, 1918).

———. *Papers*. The Newberry Library, Chicago.

———. "The Romance of a Middle-Aged Merchant and His Female Private Secretary." *Chicago Tribune*, October 4, 1884: 16.

———. *Under the Skylights* [1901] (New York: Garrett Press, 1968).

———. "The Upward Movement in Chicago." *Atlantic Monthly* LXXX (1897): 534–547.

———. *With the Procession* [1895] (Chicago: University of Chicago Press, 1965).

Garland, Hamlin. *A Son of the Middle Border* [1917], ed. Joseph B. McCullough (London: Penguin, 1995).

———. *Companions on the Trail: A Literary Chronicle* (New York: Macmillan, 1931).

———. *Crumbling Idols: Twelve Essays on Art Dealing Chiefly With Literature, Painting and the Drama* [1894], ed. Jane Johnson (Cambridge, Mass.: Belknap Press, 1960).

———. *Main-Travelled Roads* [1891] (New York: Harper & Brothers, 1922).

———. *My Friendly Contemporaries: A Literary Log* (New York: Macmillan, 1932).

———. *Roadside Meetings* (New York: Macmillan, 1930).

———. *Rose of Dutcher's Coolly* [1895], ed. Donald Pizer (Lincoln: University of Nebraska Press, 1969).

Gelfant, Blanche Housman. *The American City Novel* (Norman: University of Oklahoma Press, 1954).

Gilbert, James. *Perfect Cities: Chicago's Utopias of 1893* (Chicago: University of Chicago Press, 1991).

Giles, James R. *Confronting the Horror: The Novels of Nelson Algren* (Kent, OH: Kent State University Press, 1989).

Graham, Maryemma. "Bearing Witness in Black Chicago: A View of Selected Fiction by Richard Wright, Frank London Brown, and Ronald Fair." *CLA Journal* 33.3 (1990): 280–297.

Gutman, Herbert G. *Work, Culture, and Society in Industrializing America: Essays in American Working-Class and Social History* (New York: Alfred A. Knopf, 1976).

Guy-Sheftall, Beverly. "The Women of Bronzeville." In *On Gwendolyn Brooks: Reliant Contemplation*, ed. Stephen Caldwell Wright (Ann Arbor: University of Michigan Press, 1996), 233–245.

Hakutani, Yoshinobu. "The City and Richard Wright's Quest for Freedom." In *The City in African-American Literature*, ed. Yoshinobu Hakutani and Robert Butler (Madison: Fairleigh Dickinson University Press, 1995), 50–63.

Hallgarth, Susan A. "The Woman Who Would Be Artist in *The Song of the Lark* and *Lucy Gayheart*." In *Willa Cather: Family, Community, and History*, ed. John

J. Murphy (Provo, UT: Brigham Young University Humanities Publications Center, 1990), 169–173.

Hart, James D. *The Popular Book: A History of America's Literary Taste* (Berkeley: University of California Press, 1950).

Hawthorne, Nathaniel. *The Marble Faun: Or, the Romance of Monte Beni* [1860] (Columbus: Ohio State University Press, 1968).

Hecht, Ben. *Erik Dorn* (New York: G. P. Putnam's Sons, 1921).

Herrick, Robert. *The Common Lot* [1904] (New York: Macmillan, 1913).

———. *The Gospel of Freedom* (New York: Macmillan, 1898).

———. *A Life for a Life* (London: Macmillan, 1910).

———. *The Memoirs of an American Citizen* [1905], ed. Daniel Aaron (Cambridge, Mass.: Belknap Press, 1963).

———. *Papers.* University of Chicago Library.

———. *The Web of Life* [1900] (Upper Saddle River, NJ: Gregg Press, 1970).

Heyeck, Robin and James Woodress. "Willa Cather's Cuts and Revisions in *The Song of the Lark*." *Modern Fiction Studies* 25 (1980): 651–658.

Homberger, Eric. "Chicago and New York: Two Versions of American Modernism." In *Modernism: 1890–1930* [1976], ed. Malcolm Bradbury and James McFarlane (London: Penguin, 1991), 151–161.

Horvath, Brooke. *Understanding Nelson Algren* (Columbia: University of South Carolina Press, 2005).

Howe, Irving. *The Critical Point: On Literature and Culture* (New York: Horizon Press, 1973).

Howells, William Dean. "Certain of the Chicago School of Fiction." *North American Review* CLXXVI (1903): 734–746.

———. "The Cliff-Dwellers." *Harper's Bazar* XXVI (1893): 883.

———. *Life in Letters of William Dean Howells.* Volume I, ed. Mildred Howells (Garden City, NY: Doubleday, 1928).

———. *A Traveler from Altruria* [1894] (New York: Hill and Wang, 1957).

Hurt, James. *Writing Illinois: The Prairie, Lincoln, and Chicago* (Urbana: University of Illinois Press, 1992).

Illig, Joyce. "An Interview with Saul Bellow." In *Conversations with Saul Bellow*, ed. Gloria L. Cronin and Ben Siegel (Jackson: University Press of Mississippi, 1994), 104–112.

James, William. *The Letters of William James.* Volume II, ed. Henry James (Boston: Atlantic Monthly Press, 1920).

Jefferson, Thomas. *Notes on the State of Virginia* [1781–1782], ed. William Peden (Chapel Hill: University of North Carolina Press, 1955).

Jones, Gwendolyn. "Frank Norris's *The Pit*: 'A Romance of Chicago' and 'A Story of Chicago.'" *Frank Norris Studies* 21 (1996): 1–8.

Kaplan, Harold. *Power and Order: Henry Adams and the Naturalist Tradition in American Fiction* (Chicago: University of Chicago Press, 1981).

Kazin, Alfred. "New York from Melville to Mailer." In *Literature and the American Urban Experience: Essays on the City and Literature*, ed. Michael C. Jaye and Ann Chalmers Watts (Manchester: Manchester University Press, 1981), 81–92.

——. *On Native Grounds: An Interpretation of Modern American Prose Literature* (New York: Reynald & Hitchcock, 1942).

Kaztauskis, Antanas. "From Lithuania to the Chicago Stockyards—An Autobiography." *Independent*, August 4, 1904: 241–248.

Kipling, Rudyard. *American Notes* [1891] (New York: Arno Press, 1974).

Lattin, Patricia H. and Vernon E. "Dual Vision in Gwendolyn Brooks's *Maud Martha*." In *On Gwendolyn Brooks: Reliant Contemplation*, ed. Stephen Caldwell Wright (Ann Arbor: University of Michigan Press, 1996), 136–145.

Lawrence, Elwood P. "Fuller of Chicago: A Study in Frustration." *American Quarterly* 6.2 (1954): 137–146.

Leary, Lewis. "*Lawd Today*: Notes on Richard Wright's First/Last Novel." *CLA Journal* 15 (1972): 411–420.

Lee, Brian and Robert Reinders. "The Loss of Innocence: 1880–1914." In *Introduction to American Studies*, ed. Malcolm Bradbury and Howard Temperley (London: Longman, 1981), 176–194.

Lehan, Richard. *The City in Literature: An Intellectual and Cultural History* (Berkeley: University of California Press, 1998).

Lewin, James A. "The Radical Tradition of Algren's *Chicago: City on the Make*." *Midamerica* 19 (1992): 106–15.

Liebling, A. J. *Chicago: The Second City* (New York: Alfred A. Knopf, 1952).

"Literary West, The." Editorial. *Dial* XV (1893): 173–175.

London, Jack. *The Iron Heel* [1907] (London: Journeyman Press, 1976).

——. *The People of the Abyss* [1903] (London: Sir Isaac Pitman & Sons, 1910).

Lovett, Robert Morss. "Fuller of Chicago." *New Republic* 60 (1929): 16–18.

Lynn, Kenneth S. *The Dream of Success: A Study of the Modern American Imagination* [1955] (Westport, CT: Greenwood Press, 1972).

Marcus, Steven. "Reading the Illegible: Some Modern Representations of Urban Experience." In *Visions of the Modern City*. Second Edition, ed. William Sharpe and Leonard Wallock (Baltimore: Johns Hopkins University Press, 1987), 232–256.

Martin, Jay. *Harvests of Change: American Literature 1865–1914* (Englewood Cliffs, NJ: Prentice-Hall, 1967).

Marx, Leo. *The Machine in the Garden: Technology and the Pastoral Ideal in America* (London: Oxford University Press, 1964).

——. "The Puzzle of Anti-Urbanism in Classic American Literature." In *Literature and the American Urban Experience: Essays on the City and Literature*, ed. Michael C. Jaye and Ann Chalmers Watts (Manchester University Press, 1981), 63–80.

Masters, Edgar Lee. *Selected Poems* (New York: Macmillan, 1925).

McNamee, Tom. "Still a Writer's Town: Our Literary Giants May be Gone, but Chicago is Rich in Formidable Scribes." *Sun-Times*, April 24, 2005, Sunday Showcase: 1.

Mencken, H. L. "Civilized Chicago." *Chicago Sunday Tribune*, October 28, 1917: 5.

Miller, Donald L. *City of the Century: The Epic of Chicago and the Making of America* (New York: Simon & Schuster, 1997).

Molesworth, Charles. "Moore's 'New York' and Sandburg's 'Chicago': How Modern Can a City Be?" *William Carlos Williams Review* 14.1 (1988): 33–38.

Monroe, Harriet: *A Poet's Life: Seventy Years in a Changing World* [1938] (New York: AMS Press, 1969).

Mootry, Maria K. "'Down the Whirlwind of Good Rage': An Introduction to Gwendolyn Brooks." In *A Life Distilled: Gwendolyn Brooks, Her Poetry and Fiction*, ed. Maria K. Mootry and Gary Smith (Urbana: University of Illinois Press, 1987), 1–17.

Morrison, Toni. "City Limits, Village Values: Concepts of the Neighborhood in Black Fiction." In *Literature and the American Urban Experience: Essays on the City and Literature*, ed. Michael C. Jaye and Ann Chalmers Watts (Manchester: Manchester University Press, 1981), 35–43.

Nevius, Blake. *Robert Herrick: The Development of a Novelist* (Berkeley: University of California Press, 1962).

Norris, Frank. *The Octopus: A Story of California* [1901]. Introduction by Kevin Starr (London: Penguin, 1994).

——. *The Pit: A Story of Chicago* [1903], ed. Joseph R. McElrath, Jr. and Gwendolyn Jones (London: Penguin, 1994).

Oates, Joyce Carol. "Imaginary Cities: America." In *Literature and the American Urban Experience: Essays on the City and Literature*, ed. Michael C. Jaye and Ann Chalmers Watts (Manchester: Manchester University Press, 1981), 11–33.

Phillips, Wm. M. "Tropes and Parodies of Capitalist Biography: Carnegie's 'Gospel of Wealth' vs. Herrick's *Memoirs*." *Mosaic: A Journal for the Interdisciplinary Study of Literature* 32.1 (1999): 17–34.

Pizer, Donald. "James T. Farrell and the 1930s." In *Literature at the Barricades:*

The American Writer in the 1930s, ed. Ralph F. Bogardus and Fred Hobson (Tuscaloosa, AL: University of Alabama Press, 1982), 69–81.

———. *Realism and Naturalism in Nineteenth-Century American Literature* (New York: Russell & Russell, 1976).

———. *The Theory and Practice of American Literary Naturalism: Selected Essays and Reviews* (Carbondale: Southern Illinois University Press, 1993).

Pursell, Carroll. *The Machine in America: A Social History of Technology* (Baltimore: The Johns Hopkins University Press, 1995).

Raymer, John. "A Changing Sense of Chicago in the Works of Saul Bellow and Nelson Algren." *Old Northwest* 4 (1978): 371–383.

Rodgers, Lawrence R. "Richard Wright, Frank Marshall Davis and the Chicago Renaissance." *Langston Hughes Review* 14.1/2 (1996): 4–12.

Roe, Edward Payson. *Barriers Burned Away* [1872] (Upper Saddle River, NJ: Gregg Press, 1970).

Rotella, Carlo. *October Cities: The Redevelopment of Urban Literature* (Berkeley: University of California Press, 1998).

Royko, Mike. *Boss: Richard J. Daley of Chicago* (New York: Signet, 1971).

Ruland, Richard and Malcolm Bradbury. *From Puritanism to Postmodernism: A History of American Literature* (London: Penguin, 1992).

Sandburg, Carl. *Chicago Poems* [1916] (New York: Henry Holt, 1941).

Santayana, George. *Winds of Doctrine: Studies in Contemporary Opinion* (New York: Charles Scribner's Sons, 1913).

Sartre, Jean-Paul. "American Cities" [1955]. In *The City: American Experience*, ed. Alan Trachtenberg, Peter Neill and Peter C. Bunnell (New York: Oxford University Press, 1971), 197–205.

Scambray, Kenneth. "The Romance in Decline: Realism in Henry Blake Fuller's *The Cliff-Dwellers.*" *NDQ: North Dakota Quarterly* 46.2 (1978): 19–28.

———. *A Varied Harvest: The Life and Works of Henry Blake Fuller* (Pittsburgh: University of Pittsburgh Press, 1987).

Schlesinger, Arthur. *Paths to the Present* (New York: Macmillan, 1949).

Shiffman, Daniel. "Ethnic Competitors in *Studs Lonigan.*" *Melus* 24.3 (1999): 67–79.

Siegel, Adrienne. *The Image of the American City in Popular Literature, 1820–1870* (Port Washington, NY: Kennikat Press, 1981).

Sinclair, Upton. *The Autobiography of Upton Sinclair* (New York: Harcourt, Brace & World, 1962).

———. *The Jungle* [1906] (Harmondsworth: Penguin, 1965).

———. *My Lifetime in Letters* (Columbia: University of Missouri Press, 1960).

Smith, Carl S. *Chicago and the American Literary Imagination 1880–1920* (Chicago: University of Chicago Press, 1984).

Smith, Henry Nash. *Virgin Land: The American West as Symbol and Myth* (New York: Vintage, 1950).

Spender, Stephen. "Poetry and the Modern City." In *Literature and the American Urban Experience: Essays on the City and Literature*, ed. Michael C. Jaye and Ann Chalmers Watts (Manchester: Manchester University Press, 1981), 45–49.

St. Clair, Janet. "Chicago's Tutors: The Humorous Columnists of the 1880's and 90's." *American Transcendental Quarterly* 37 (1988): 237–248.

Steevens, George Warrington. *The Land of the Dollar*. Fourth Edition (Edinburgh: William Blackwood, 1900).

Steffens, Lincoln. *The Shame of the Cities* [1904] (New York: Peter Smith, 1948).

Stevens, Sufjan. "Come On! Feel the Illinoise!" *Illinois*. Asthmatic Kitty Records, 2005.

Strauss, Anselm, *Images of the American City* [1961] (New Brunswick, NJ: Transaction, 1976).

Street, Julian. *Abroad at Home: American Ramblings, Observations, and Adventures of Julian Street* (New York: Century, 1914).

Stronks, James B. "A Realist Experiments with Impressionism: Hamlin Garland's 'Chicago Studies.'" *American Literature* 36.1 (1964): 38–52.

Sullivan, Louis B. *The Autobiography of an Idea* [1924] (New York: Dover, 1956).

Swanson, Jeffrey. "'Flesh, Fish or Fowl': Henry Blake Fuller's Attitudes Toward Realism and Romanticism." *American Literary Realism 1870–1910* 7.3 (1974): 195–210.

Terkel, Studs. *Chicago* (New York: Pantheon, 1986).

Trachtenberg, Alan. *The Incorporation of America: Culture and Society in the Guilded Age* (New York: Hill and Wang, 1982).

Turner, Frederick Jackson. *The Frontier in American History* [essays first collected in this form: 1920]. With a Foreword by Ray Allen Billington (Malabar, FL: Robert E. Krieger, 1985).

Van Wienen, Mark. "Taming the Socialist: Carl Sandburg's Chicago Poems and its Critics." *American Literature* 63.1 (1991): 89–103.

Weimer, David R. *The City as Metaphor* (New York: Random House, 1966).

Weiss, Richard. *The American Myth of Success: From Horatio Alger to Norman Vincent Peale* (New York: Basic, 1969).

Wells, H. G. *Anticipations: Of the Reaction of Mechanical and Scientific Progress Upon Human Life and Thought* (New York: Dover, 1999).

White, Morton and Lucia White. *The Intellectual Versus the City: From Thomas Jefferson to Frank Lloyd Wright* (Cambridge, Mass.: Harvard University Press, The MIT Press, 1962).

Williams, Kenny J. *In the City of Men: Another Story of Chicago* (Nashville, TN: Townsend Press, 1974).

——. *Prairie Voices: A Literary History of Chicago from the Frontier to 1893* (Nashville, TN: Townsend Press, 1980).

——. "The World of Satin-Legs, Mrs. Sallie, and the Blackstone Rangers: The Restricted Chicago of Gwendolyn Brooks." In *A Life Distilled: Gwendolyn Brooks, Her Poetry and Fiction*, ed. Maria K. Mootry and Gary Smith (Urbana: University of Illinois Press, 1987), 47–70.

Wordsworth, William. "Composed upon Westminster Bridge, September 3, 1802." In *The Norton Anthology of English Literature*. Seventh Edition. Volume 2, ed. M. H. Abrams and Stephen Greenblatt (New York: W. W. Norton, 2000), 296.

Wright, Richard. *American Hunger* (New York: Harper & Row, 1977).

——. "How 'Bigger' Was Born" [1940]. In *Native Son* (New York: Harper & Row, 1987), vii–xxxiv.

——. *Lawd Today* (New York: Walker, 1963).

——. *Native Son* [1940] (New York: Harper & Row, 1987).

Ziff, Larzer. *The American 1890s: Life and Times of a Lost Generation* (Lincoln: University of Nebraska Press, 1966).

Index

www.ingramcontent.com/pod-product-compliance
Lightning Source LLC
Chambersburg PA
CBHW030251130626

46549CB00002B/487